P9-DBL-703

OCT 1 4 2016

Bristow Middle School
Library Media Center
34 Bristow Street
West Hartford, CT 06119

# COSTA RICA
## in Pictures

VGS

Tom Streissguth

Lerner Publications Company

# Contents

Lerner Publishing Group realizes that current information and statistics quickly become out of date. To extend the usefulness of the Visual Geography Series, we developed www.vgsbooks.com, a website offering links to up-to-date information, as well as in-depth material, on a wide variety of subjects. All of the websites listed on www.vgsbooks.com have been carefully selected by researchers at Lerner Publishing Group. However, Lerner Publishing Group is not responsible for the accuracy or suitability of the material on any website other than <www.lernerbooks.com>. It is recommended that students using the Internet be supervised by a parent or teacher. Links on www.vgsbooks.com will be regularly reviewed and updated as needed.

Copyright © 2004 by Tom Streissguth

All rights reserved. International copyright secured. No part of this book may be reproduced, stored in a retrieval system, or transmitted in any form or by any means— electronic, mechanical, photocopying, recording, or otherwise—without the prior written permission of Lerner Publications Company, except for the inclusion of brief quotations in an acknowledged review.

Lerner Publications Company
A division of Lerner Publishing Group
241 First Avenue North
Minneapolis, MN 55401 U.S.A.

Website address: www.lernerbooks.com

web enhanced @ www.vgsbooks.com

Library of Congress Cataloging-in-Publication Data

Streissguth, Thomas, 1958–
   Costa Rica in pictures / Tom Streissguth.—Rev. & expanded.
      p.   cm. — (Visual geography series)
   Includes bibliographical references and index.
   Contents: The land. History and government. The people. Cultural life. The economy.
   ISBN: 0-8225-1168-1 (lib. bdg. : alk. paper)
   1. Costa Rica—Juvenile literature. [1. Costa Rica] I. Title. II. Series: Visual geography series
(Minneapolis, Minn.)
F1543.2.S77  2004
972.86—dc22

Manufactured in the United States of America
1  2  3  4  5  6  - BP - 09  08  07  06  05  04

2003023460

Bristow Middle School

3254716006823
972.86 Str
Costa Rica in pictures

# INTRODUCTION

The nation of Costa Rica (Spanish for "rich coast") lies in Central America between the Caribbean Sea to the east and the Pacific Ocean to the west. In modern times, Costa Rica is a unique success story. In a region plagued by poverty, Costa Rica boasts a large middle class and a generally prosperous society. While neighboring nations have suffered from political instability, Costa Ricans have held regular national elections since the late nineteenth century.

The nation traces its history to ancient times. Indigenous, or native, peoples have lived in Costa Rica for thousands of years. European explorers and settlers arrived in the sixteenth century. Afterward, Costa Rica became a colony of Spain—a region ruled by the faraway Spanish nation. Spanish settlers brought their traditions and religion (Catholicism) to Costa Rica. Spanish became the nation's official language.

Colonial Costa Rica lay far from important trade routes, and for centuries, the colony remained isolated and sparsely populated. Costa Rica

began its modern history as one of the smallest and poorest nations in the Western Hemisphere. At the end of the nineteenth century, Costa Rica had few roads and only a single railroad line. Its cities and ports remained small, and industry was nonexistent. The Costa Rican economy depended on exporting agricultural products, particularly coffee, to other nations.

Many Spanish settlers in Costa Rica, who were white, intermarried with indigenous peoples. Their offspring—people of mixed blood— were called mestizos. Europeans also brought Africans to Central America to work as slaves, primarily along the Caribbean coast. Immigrants from northern Europe began to arrive in Costa Rica during the nineteenth century. In modern times, Costa Rica attracts newcomers from other Central American countries, South America, and the United States. Costa Rica has a reputation as a peaceful country and serves as a haven for refugees from other strife-torn countries in the region.

Within Latin America (the nations south of the United States), Costa Rica holds a reputation as a society that takes good care of its people, with little class and ethnic conflict. Universal public education has been the rule in Costa Rica since 1869. In the twentieth century, the country expanded its public health and social security (public welfare) systems. Although these systems have strained the government budget, the programs have paid off. Costa Rica has the best health statistics and highest life expectancy figures in Central America.

Among the most valuable resources of modern Costa Rica is its physical landscape. National parks and preserves cover about one-quarter of the nation's total land area. The country has preserved (protected from development) a higher percentage of its land than any other nation on earth. Its forests, mountains, volcanoes, and seacoasts draw visitors from all over the globe, and tourism has become a mainstay of the Costa Rican economy.

Increased tourism, however, has given rise to environmental problems and social tension. For instance, the construction of hotels and other tourist facilities has destroyed wilderness and seacoasts. In many areas, this process has uprooted families and brought the woes of traffic, noise, and pollution.

Costa Rica also faces economic problems such as high foreign debt, inflation (rising prices), and unemployment. Government officials are hard put to find solutions to these problems. Yet Costa Ricans draw on a long-ingrained sense of optimism and independence to meet these challenges. Costa Ricans are confident that they can overcome new problems as they have overcome others in the past.

Standing at the buttress, or exposed root trunk, of a ceiba tree, **ecotourists** gaze up at the canopy of a Costa Rican rain forest. Tourism has helped the Costa Rican economy, but it has caused several problems for the country's natural and social environments.

# THE LAND

Costa Rica occupies part of the Central American isthmus, a narrow strip of land between the Caribbean Sea and the Pacific Ocean. Nicaragua borders Costa Rica on the north, and Panama lies to the southeast. The eastern coast of Costa Rica borders the Caribbean, while the Pacific Ocean lies along the western coast. Covering 19,929 square miles (51,616 square kilometers), Costa Rica is slightly smaller than the state of West Virginia. Within Central America, only El Salvador and Belize are smaller.

Despite its small size, Costa Rica boasts a great diversity of landscapes. Tropical rain forests stand along both coasts. The eastern coast features low-lying coastal plains, with humidity and high temperatures year-round. Through the center of the country, a long chain of mountains towers above thickly forested valleys. Near the center of this chain is the Central Valley with rich, fertile soil. The Pacific coastline features steep highlands that isolate the region from the rest of the country. Costa Rica's varying physical regions have allowed a great diversity of mammal, bird, insect, and plant species to flourish.

## ▶ The Caribbean Lowlands

The level Caribbean Lowlands are a region of year-round rainfall, high temperatures and high humidity, mangrove swamps, and a long strip of flat seacoast. The major rivers of the Caribbean Lowlands—the Chirripó, Tortuguero, Reventazón, Pacuare, Chirripó Atlántico, and Estrella—all flow eastward to the sea. Originating in the mountains, these rivers wind through humid rain forests and extensive banana plantations that date to the late nineteenth century. In the south, the Sixaola River forms a short boundary with Panama. The San Juan River marks the nation's northern border with Nicaragua.

## ▶ The Mountains and Central Valley

A chain of volcanic mountain ranges runs down the center of Costa Rica. The northernmost mountains belong to the Guanacaste Range, followed to the southeast by the Tilarán, Central, and Talamanca ranges. A large lake, Lake Arenal, sits at the border of the Guanacaste and Tilarán ranges.

The Talamanca Range, running from central Costa Rica to the Panama border, is the nation's largest, most remote, and highest mountain range. Chirripó Grande, the highest peak in this range, reaches 12,530 feet (3,819 meters), making it the highest point in Costa Rica as well. The General River and its tributaries (small feeder rivers) run down from the tall slopes to the Pacific Ocean.

The ranges feature several active volcanoes that regularly eject ash, smoke, and glowing red lava. The Arenal Volcano rises near Lake Arenal. In the Central Range, Poás and Irazú are also active volcanoes and are the main features of two national parks. Although volcanoes have brought death and devastation to Costa Rican cities at times, the erupting volcanoes have also helped the country by depositing fertile volcanic soil into the valleys.

The Central Valley begins on the western side of the Central Range. The valley covers only about 600 square miles (1,554 sq. km), yet it is home to about two-thirds of the nation's population. The valley's rich volcanic soil and mild climate have encouraged settlement. It is the site of the Costa Rican capital, San José, and four of the country's five largest cities. The region remains the economic and cultural heart of the country.

The peak of Chirripó Grande, Costa Rica's highest point, rises up from the Talamanca Range, touching the clouds.

A rancho, or ranch, sits on the rugged terrain of the **Guanacaste Province.** The region is home to most of Costa Rica's cattle ranchos.

## Guanacaste and the Pacific Coast

In the far northwest corner of the country, the Pacific Ocean meets a rugged, curving coastline. In this region are the Guanacaste Province and the hilly Nicoya Peninsula, both the site of large cattle ranches and beach resorts. Here the Tempisque and Tenorio Rivers flow south to the Gulf of Nicoya. From the shores of the gulf, the province of Puntarenas stretches south along the Pacific coast to the border of Panama. Tropical forests and a series of small, sheltered bays line the coast. In the southwest is the Osa Peninsula, largely separated from the mainland by the Dulce Gulf.

## Climate

Although small in area and lying entirely within the tropics (a zone near the equator of yearlong warm temperatures), Costa Rica experiences a great variety of weather. Two basic seasons, wet and dry, alternate during the year. The dry season lasts from December to April, while the wet season lasts through spring, summer, and fall.

In the Caribbean Lowlands, prevailing northeasterly winds pass over the warm waters of the sea, bringing heavy rainfall to the coast as well as to the eastern slopes of the highlands. Heavy rains fall all year long, even during the so-called dry season. In fact, rainfall here is the heaviest in the country, averaging 150 to 200 inches (381 to 508 centimeters) a year. Temperatures are also high year-round. Daytime highs frequently reach 100°F (38°C). At night, temperatures fall to about 60°F to 70°F (16°C to 21°C).

The higher elevations of the Central Valley and the mountains that block coastal rainstorms have a drier, more moderate climate throughout the year. Daytime temperatures average about 75°F (24°C), with lows of about 59°F (15°C). About 70 inches (178 cm) of rain fall each year.

The Pacific coast has more marked wet and dry seasons than does the Central Valley. Rainfall on this coast averages about 130 inches (330 cm) a year. Rainfall increases to the south, where daytime temperatures range from 77°F to 100°F (25°C to 38°C).

## ◉ Flora and Fauna

Scientists estimate that up to one million species of plants, animals, and insects live in Costa Rica (about 5 percent of all the species on earth). There are nine opossum species, three of the four known species of anteaters, and two varieties of rare tree sloths. Armadillos and bats share remote stretches of forest with four species of monkeys: squirrel monkeys, white-faced capuchin monkeys, spider monkeys, and mantled howler monkeys. The coati, kinkajou, and

**A white-faced capuchin monkey** lounges in a tree.

### THE SHY MONKEYS OF COSTA RICA

Costa Rica is home to four different species of monkey: the white-faced capuchin, mantled howler monkey, spider monkey, and squirrel monkey, or titi, which survives only in Costa Rica's southern Pacific coastal area. The monkeys live in troops of a few dozen members and range over a wide area, looking for food. The arrival of thousands of curious tourists in national parks and preserves, however, has driven many monkey troops deeper into the forests and mountains, where they can roam and search for food undisturbed. As a result, although the Costa Rican monkey population holds steady, monkeys have become increasingly shy and hard to spot.

Cocos Island, the largest uninhabited island in the world, sits 364 miles (586 km) off Costa Rica's Pacific coast. It was a favorite stop for pirates and voyagers in the seventeenth and eighteenth centuries. A national park, the island receives about 276 inches (701 cm) of rain every year, which supports a thriving rain forest and freshwater springs. More than seventy insect species and seventy plant species can only be found on the island. The waters around the island are home to coral, fish, and sharks. Visit www.vgsbooks.com to learn more about Cocos Island.

cacomistle are small mammals belonging to the raccoon family. Among cats, Costa Rica hosts the jaguar, puma, jaguarundi, ocelot, yellow margay, and rare oncilla. These carnivores (meat eaters) hunt rodents and small mammals, including otters, rabbits, and weasels.

Costa Rica is also home to more than eight hundred species of birds. Many varieties of hummingbirds live throughout the country. Five kinds of tinamous, a small and rare tailless bird, live and feed mainly near the ground. Black vultures, turkey vultures, and yellow-headed vultures commonly feed on carrion (dead animals). Raptor (hunting) species include ospreys, hawks, kites, eagles, falcons, and caracaras. Along the seacoasts, the most common birds are pelicans, egrets, petrels, herons, and spoonbills. Inland, rivers and lakes are the favorite haunts of cormorants and anhingas. The seacoasts and

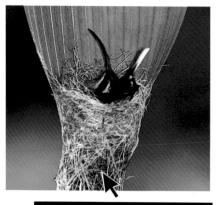

**A long-tailed hermit hummingbird** makes its home in a cocoonlike nest. Costa Rican **wild orchids** grow in the rain forest.

Costa Rican waters contain **coral reefs and colorful fish. Giant sea turtles** nest along Costa Rica's shores. The Costa Rican government is making efforts to protect the living reefs and turtle nesting grounds, but tourism and overbuilding remain a threat to these animals and their habitats.

coastal waters also provide homes for fish, giant sea turtles, humpback whales, dolphins, and the West Indian manatee, a large, herbivorous (plant-eating) aquatic mammal.

Costa Rica's rain forests are home to a wide variety of trees, shrubs, and vines. The tree branches form a high canopy over the smaller plants below. Costa Rica has some eight hundred species of ferns, the most common plant in rain forest areas, and more than thirty types of heliconias, also known as bird of paradise. Bromeliads and orchids are epiphytes, plants that grow on tree branches or vines and take in moisture from the air and rain. The big leaves of the *sombrilla de pobre,* or "poor man's umbrella," can grow to 5 feet (1.5 meters) across.

## ⊙ Natural Resources

Costa Rica has small deposits of coal, but no oil or natural gas. It has small and isolated veins of silver ore, as well as gold deposits on the Nicoya Peninsula. Minerals such as diatomite, sand, clay, and stone are used in industry and construction. The tropical forests provide valuable timber, although overcutting has greatly depleted this resource. The country's many fast-flowing rivers provide the basic fuel for hydroelectrical plants. The power of the rushing water is used to create electricity, which Costa Rica exports to some of its neighbors.

## Environmental Issues

Costa Rica faces a serious problem in the form of deforestation—the destruction of its thick rain forests. Most of the nation's original rain forest has been cleared for agriculture to create banana and coffee plantations, farms, and pasture for livestock. Even in areas designated as off-limits to logging, some logging continues illegally. In the late twentieth century, forests were being cut at a rate of 193 square miles (500 sq. km) per year, one of the highest rates of deforestation in the world.

Deforestation has led to heavy soil erosion, a process by which rain washes away topsoil, because there are no tree roots left to hold the soil in place. The eroded topsoil flows into rivers, eventually clogging them up and hurting the plants, fish, and other animals that make their homes there. What's more, logging also reduces habitat for forest-dwelling plants and animals.

The Costa Rican government has recently set up the Environmental Services Payment Program. Under this program, the government pays landowners to plant trees that are native to Costa Rica in deforested areas. Examples include balsa, mahogany, and cieba trees. This program is meant to protect and reverse the destruction of the rain forest.

The plantations and farms that have replaced the forests also damage the environment. For instance, growers use pesticides (chemicals that kill insects) to protect banana and coffee plants from insects. However, these chemicals run off into rivers and lakes, polluting the water and harming the plants and animals that live there.

Many cities in Costa Rica have grown rapidly, and this urban growth has brought environmental problems. Cars, taxis, buses, motorcycles, and motor scooters in San José and other cities create heavy air pollution. Factories and processing plants also pollute the air and water. In addition, the construction of new homes and office buildings destroys natural habitat for animals and plant species.

In the last half of the twentieth century, Costa Rica set aside dozens of national parks, biological reserves, and wildlife refuges to help protect

### THE CABO BLANCO RESERVE

The preservation of land in Costa Rica found important friends in Nils and Karen Wessberg, Swedish immigrants who arrived in 1955 to build a home on the Nicoya Peninsula. After seeing much of the area rain forest destroyed for development, the Wessbergs spent several years raising money to create the 3,000-acre (1,215-hectare) Cabo Blanco Reserve. Visit www.vgsbooks.com for links to more information.

A waterfall cascades in the lush **La Amistad Biosphere Reserve.** In addition to providing protection for rain forest, plants and animals, the reserve also protects a major share of Costa Rica's freshwater.

plant and animal life. In fact, more than 25 percent of the country has been protected from new construction and the clearing of land for farming. Santa Rosa National Park, the first of these parks, was established in 1971. The largest reserve, La Amistad Biosphere Reserve, stretches across the border with Panama in southeastern Costa Rica. Within Costa Rica, La Amistad covers 1.5 million acres (607,000 hectares), or about 12 percent of the country. Santa Rosa and Guanacaste National Park, both in the northwest Guanacaste Province, have become important sites for the preservation and study of animal species facing extinction.

## Cities

Costa Rica's population is split between urban and rural areas. Approximately 60 percent of Costa Ricans live in cities. The rest of the nation's people live in rural areas. The major cities are San José, Puerto Limón, Alajuela, Cartago, and Heredia.

SAN JOSÉ (population 309,672), the capital and largest city of Costa Rica, was founded around 1738. Located in the Central Valley, this sprawling city was the second capital of Costa Rica (nearby Cartago was the first), but it has long surpassed its neighboring cities in size and importance.

Costa Ricans and tourists gather in **San José's Plaza de la Cultura** (Culture Plaza) in the heart of the city. The Teatro Nacional, Costa Rica's National Theater *(left),* is an important feature of the plaza and is revered by many Costa Ricans. For links to websites about Costa Rican cities, regions, weather, as well as plants and animals, visit www.vgsbooks. com.

Fueled by coffee exports, the city prospered in the late 1800s. It adopted modern advances: electricity in private homes, public telephones, and universal education for men and women. During this era, the city also built a national public library, a national theater, and a national museum. It attracted artists and performers from Europe and the United States and became a Latin American cultural center.

San José became the economic heart of both Costa Rica and Central America. Banks and other private companies, many of them foreign owned, made their Central American headquarters in the capital. In the mid-twentieth century, the city's planners tore down older, dilapidated neighborhoods, built new apartment blocks, and laid down orderly street plans.

In the late twentieth century, San José's population exploded. Traffic congestion choked the streets, and high-rises made of glass and steel replaced older buildings, homes, and shops made of stone. While busy street markets survived in downtown San José, shopping malls, chain stores, and fast-food restaurants appeared in the city and its sprawling suburbs.

Despite the growth, impressive old landmarks have survived, as have several parks and plazas that give residents a respite from noise, air pollution, and dense traffic. The National Theater, built in the 1890s, gives a prominent stage to music, theater, and ballet companies. The National Museum, the Pre-Columbian Gold Museum, and the Museum of Jade compete for attention with private art galleries and exhibitions. Josefinos (the people of San José) also enjoy nightclubs, coffee shops, restaurants, and cyber-cafés.

PUERTO LIMÓN (population 56,719) sits on a rise of coastal land and is the biggest city on the Caribbean coast. It was founded in 1871 as an entry point for Afro-Caribbean laborers hired to work on the Atlantic Railway, built to link San José to the Atlantic coast. Its culture draws heavily on both African and Caribbean traditions. On October 12, the people of Puerto Limón commemorate the 1492 landing of Christopher Columbus, the first European explorer to reach the Western Hemisphere. People celebrate with parades, dancing, and a festive carnival.

ALAJUELA (population 42,889), the capital of Alajuela Province, lies 12 miles (19 km) northwest of San José. Founded in 1782 as Villa Hermosa, the city has long prided itself as the birthplace of Juan Santamaría, the hero of Costa Rica's victory over an army of foreigners in 1856. A museum dedicated to Santamaría's life attracts visitors interested in Costa Rican history, and a city park has also been named for him. Each year on April 11, Alajuela commemorates the 1856 Battle of Rivas, in which Santamaría died while fighting foreign armies led by U.S. adventurer William Walker.

CARTAGO (population 38,363) was founded in 1563. It was the country's first capital city. It remains a Catholic religious center. Pilgrims—people who travel to holy places—come to Cartago from all over Costa Rica. The Basilica of Our Lady of the Angels, a church dedicated to Costa Rica's patron saint (protector), towers over the city. Las Ruinas de Cartago is another well-known landmark. It consists of the ruins of a church located within the city's central park. Built in 1575, the church survived many earthquakes until it was leveled by an earthquake in 1910.

HEREDIA Settled in 1706 on the slopes of the Barva Volcano, Heredia (population 30,000) lies in the heart of an important coffee-growing region. Also known as the City of Flowers, Heredia has extensive green spaces and a large central park. The National Autonomous University brings a large student population to this town. The city's colonial past survives in old adobe (mud brick) homes and a famous church built in the 1760s.

# HISTORY AND GOVERNMENT

Historians and archaeologists (scholars who study early human cultures) have dated human habitation of Costa Rica and the rest of Central America as far back as 12,000 B.C. Some historians think the ancestors of Central America's first residents wandered south along the Pacific coast from Alaska, after crossing a land bridge that once linked North America to Asia. Scientists, however, are exploring other theories on the origins and arrival of Central America's first inhabitants.

The earliest humans in the region were nomadic hunter-gatherers, people who moved from one region to the next in search of food such as fruits, roots, and animals. These early inhabitants built homes of bark, made clothing from animal hides, and crafted tools from stone and clay.

By 1000 B.C., early Central Americans were living in permanent villages. Several distinct tribal nations had emerged. Heading each such group was a chieftain, known as a cacique. Indigenous peoples traded

with each other and with other tribes to the north and south, through-out present-day Mexico and the Pacific and Atlantic coasts of South America. To travel from place to place, they used seagoing boats as well as footpaths that crisscrossed the region's mountains and forests.

The indigenous peoples of Costa Rica included the Chorotega, Huetar, Térraba, Boruca, Coctu, and Corobici, as well as the Bribrí and the Cabecares of the Talamanca Range. Large settlements in the Guanacaste and Nicoya regions numbered several hundred households each. Most groups lived by hunting and by growing corn and other crops. While they had no written language, these groups spoke a great variety of indigenous languages, with most using Huetar, the language of the Central Valley. Tribes practiced traditional religions, involving spirit worship and ancestor worship. Priests called shamans acted as both healers and spiritual leaders.

Different groups had different customs and lifestyles. In the Diquís region of southern Costa Rica, people lived in fortified villages,

## MYSTERIOUS SPHERES

Costa Rica's southern Pacific region holds an archaeological mystery in the form of hundreds of round stone balls *(bolas)* that litter the region's rain forests and riverbeds. Beginning about 200 B.C., native artisans cut pieces of granodiorite, a hard volcanic stone, from quarries. By chipping, scraping, and smoothing, they formed the stone into balls, some as tall as an adult human being and weighing as much as 16 tons (14.5 metric tons). The spheres were carved at the quarries and then moved as far as 18 miles (30 km) away. No one knows for sure why they were made, although they may have decorated native religious sites or marked the location of the sun or moon or the points of the compass.

Many of the spheres have since been moved from their first resting places. Some sit in the front of public buildings, while others are used as garden and lawn ornaments at Costa Rican houses. A few remain in their original homes, silently guarding the secret of their origin and purpose.

Several of the **Costa Rican spheres** are on display at the Museo Nacional (National Museum) in San José. The purpose of the ancient spheres remains a mystery.

surrounded by earthen and log barriers. This area became an important gold mining center, a fact that may have brought raids by and warfare with other groups. At their cemeteries and ceremonial sites, the people of the region left behind carved stone globes, perfectly round and ranging in size from a few inches to several feet across.

In the city of Guayabo, east of the Central Valley, people drew water from aqueducts, long, hollow pipes made of stone slabs. The aqueducts carried water to the village from nearby rivers. The streets of Guayabo were paved with sawn logs. The city died out around A.D. 1400, probably during a conflict with neighboring tribes. The Nicoya region to the west had several busy ports, and the inhabitants used oceangoing boats to trade with people in other settlements along the Pacific coast.

## Europeans in Costa Rica

On September 8, 1502, during his fourth and final voyage to the Americas, the Italian navigator Christopher Columbus arrived with a fleet of four ships off modern-day Puerto Limón. Searching for a western route to Asia, Columbus explored the coast of Central America. On his first voyage to the Americas, ten years earlier, Columbus thought he had landed on an island of the East Indies, or Southeast Asia, so he called the native people Indians. That name came to apply to all natives in the Western Hemisphere.

Because the Indians had gold-covered mirrors and jewelry and told stories of local gold mines, Columbus believed he had found a land rich in gold. His reports back to the king and queen of Spain, who had sponsored his voyages, inspired further explorations of the area. Later explorers, who also believed the region held great mineral wealth, named it Costa Rica. The Spanish adopted Costa Rica as the official name of the region in 1539.

A ship full of Spanish colonists, led by Diego de Nicuesa, landed in Costa Rica in 1506. The region's rough terrain made farming difficult, however, and local diseases such as yellow fever and malaria sickened the colonists. Local indigenous tribes also attacked the Spaniards, burned their crops, and drove them away. Nevertheless, Spanish explorers and colonists continued to arrive in Costa Rica.

**Navigator Christopher Columbus** set anchor in the bay off Cariari (present-day Puerto Limón) in 1502. Prior to the arrival of Columbus and other Europeans, native peoples had been living in the Costa Rica region for thousands of years. If you would like to learn more about Costa Rica's spheres and early history, visit www.vgsbooks.com.

In 1522 a Spaniard named Gil González Dávila explored the interior of Costa Rica, starting from the Gulf of Nicoya. More settlements were formed, this time on the Pacific coast. González demanded tribute, or payment, in the form of gold and pearls from the Chorotega tribe. He also forced many Indians to convert to Catholicism, the religion of Spain. Indigenous groups continued to attack Spanish settlements, and settlers continued to die of disease. The first settlements failed on both the Atlantic and Pacific coasts.

To attract new settlers to its struggling colonies in this region, Spain established a program called the *encomienda* system. An encomienda was an estate given to a settler, who also received the legal right to use local native peoples to work the land. The settlers promised eventual freedom to the native peoples but in most cases held them as permanent unpaid laborers—essentially slaves. Many native peoples died from harsh treatment, backbreaking labor, and diseases the settlers had brought from Europe. The settlers soon found their lands going to waste and their farms destitute. In 1542 Spain abolished the encomienda system and replaced it with the *repartimiento*, a system that required male Indians between ages sixteen and sixty to work one week per month on the estates of local settlers.

In 1561 a leader named Juan de Cavallón arrived with more Spanish colonists from Guatemala and Nicaragua to the north. This expedition established Garcimunoz, the first successful settlement in Costa Rica. About a year later, an explorer named Juan Vásquez de Coronado moved this group to the Central Valley. There, he founded Cartago as the Costa Rican capital in 1563.

Coronado made peace with a local Indian chief, who persuaded several other chiefs to cooperate with the Spaniards. Despite this agreement, many settlers, seeking land for their estates, attacked the indigenous people, who died in fierce battles with the colonists. Other native peoples died of disease. Many remaining tribes fled from the valleys and coasts into the nearly inaccessible Talamanca Range. Those Indians who did not flee were enslaved by the colonists.

In 1565 the king of Spain appointed Coronado as the first official governor of Costa Rica. But Coronado died on a return trip to America from Spain the same year. In 1570 Costa Rica became part of a larger colonial unit, the Captaincy General of Guatemala, covering southern Mexico and most of Central America, with its capital in Guatemala City.

## Colonial Life

Costa Rica proved difficult for the Spanish to govern. Natural obstacles, including high mountains and thick tropical forests, hampered settlement. Spanish colonists continued to struggle with disease.

The **ruins of the first Catholic church** Spaniards built in Costa Rica as part of their encomienda system. The system did not work well in Costa Rica, because few Spaniards were willing to move to the area and native laborers often sickened and died. Link to information about the encomienda system at www.vgsbooks.com.

Indigenous people continued to die out. Some African slaves were imported to work the land, but little of the land was suitable for farming. Costa Rica lay far from colonial administrative centers in Mexico and Guatemala. Communications were poor, and the colony developed independently of direct control by Spain and the distant Spanish governors.

Eventually, Spanish settlers founded the towns of Nicoya and Espiritu Santo on the Pacific coast. A few settlers mined small gold deposits, found along creek beds and hillsides. But by the seventeenth century, the gold had run out, and the colony was struggling. Farming families eked out a bare existence on small holdings. Costa Ricans also had to contend with natural disasters, such as the 1723 eruption of the Irazú Volcano, which buried Cartago in ash.

Costa Rica remained a poor outpost in Central America throughout the seventeenth and eighteenth centuries. Unlike other Latin American colonies, it had no large social divisions between landowners and common laborers. It had no industry or large-scale mining. Nearly all the colonists worked their own small patches of land.

The Spanish established new towns in Costa Rica's Central Valley in the early eighteenth century. Heredia was founded in the early 1700s.

Around 1738 a group of settlers from Cartago founded the city of San José. In 1782 another group of colonists established Villa Hermosa.

Conflict with the indigenous tribes continued through the eighteenth century. On several occasions, settlers raided the Talamanca region, which had become a refuge for indigenous people escaping forced labor. These raids ended in the forced resettlement of many indigenous groups to the Central Valley.

At the same time, Miskitos, the children of escaped African slaves who had married indigenous people, became a sizable community along the Atlantic coast of Costa Rica and Nicaragua. Through the late seventeenth and eighteenth centuries, the Miskitos vied with the Costa Rican governor for control of the coast.

Costa Rican trade was limited, mostly consisting of mules and tobacco exchanged with nearby colonies. But in 1808, the first coffee plants arrived in Costa Rica from Jamaica, a British colony in the Caribbean Sea. Soon Costa Ricans were growing and exporting coffee themselves. Other plantations produced chocolate, a delicacy popular in Europe and throughout the American colonies. But pirates in search of money and treasure raided these plantations constantly, reducing the Atlantic coast to a state of near lawlessness.

## Independence

From the capital in Guatemala City, Costa Rica was the most distant part of the Captaincy General of Guatemala. The influence of Spain's colonial government, Spanish law, and the Catholic Church remained weak in Costa Rica.

In the meantime, wars in Europe brought about turmoil in the mother country of Spain. In 1808 France invaded Spain and overthrew its monarch. Soon afterward, the Spanish colonies, inspired by the drive for independence in North America and revolutions against European kings, sought their own freedom. Latin American rebels clashed with Spanish troops, eventually ending Spanish control in the Americas. Mexico declared independence from Spain in April 1821. On September 15, in Guatemala City, the Central American territories—Guatemala, Nicaragua, El Salvador, Costa Rica, and Honduras—declared themselves free of Spain as well.

On October 13, 1821, a full month after the event, news of this declaration finally reached Costa Rica's Central Valley. Still one of the poorest and most neglected regions of Latin America, Costa Rica was home to only about sixty thousand inhabitants at the time.

Costa Rican leaders debated whether or not to join an empire being formed by Mexican leader Agustín Iturbide. They had two other choices: to become a completely independent nation or to join the new province of Colombia headed by Simón Bolívar, a Venezuelan general and a leader in the fight for Latin American independence.

The debate in Costa Rica developed into a civil war. A group called the Monarchists, based in Cartago, favored joining the Mexican Empire, while a group called Republicans, based in San José, favored total independence. On April 5, 1823, a battle between Monarchists and Republicans in the mountains separating Cartago and San José left twenty men dead. The proindependence Republicans won the battle.

Several days before the battle, Guatemala, Nicaragua, El Salvador, Costa Rica, and Honduras had founded the United Provinces of Central America. According to its constitution, each member of this union would elect its own head of state and send representatives to a federal congress in Guatemala City.

In December 1823, Costa Rica drafted its own constitution, known as the Pacto de Concordia. The constitution abolished slavery but allowed only a small class of male property owners, all descended from Spanish settlers, to vote. These voters elected Juan Mora Fernandez as Costa Rica's first head of state. The constitution also stated that the capital would be rotated among the four principal cities of Cartago, San José, Heredia, and Alajuela. In 1825 Costa Rica annexed the Guanacaste Province, which had seceded (withdrawn) from Nicaragua that year.

**Workers spread coffee beans for drying** at a Costa Rican coffee plantation in the 1800s. While the Pacto de Concordia of 1823 made slavery illegal in Costa Rica, many workers labored under slaverylike conditions.

José Rafael Gallegos was elected president in a hotly contested election in 1833. An unpopular and unwilling leader, Gallegos soon resigned. At this time, Costa Rica was suffering armed conflict between political factions, friction among different social and ethnic groups, and rising crime. Gallegos was succeeded by Braulio Carrillo Colina, who imposed a strict rule on the country—his word became the law. Carrillo levied taxes for the building of new roads, invested in trade with Europe, and put down Miskito raids on Costa Rican towns and settlements. New coffee plantations were established. Coffee growers sold their beans directly to merchants in Great Britain, and very quickly, coffee became Costa Rica's most valuable crop.

## ◗ The Rise of San José

Carrillo's energetic rule made San José, where he enjoyed the most influence and popularity, the political and financial center of Costa Rica. But the growing power of San José bred resentment among the other three principal towns. Heredia, Alajuela, and Cartago formed a league to battle San José and Carrillo for control of the country. Called the War of the League, the fighting ended with the Treaty of Virilla and the victory of San José. Carrillo then established that city as Costa Rica's permanent capital.

Carrillo left office in 1837 but staged a coup (overthrow) of his successor the next year. He then proclaimed himself president for life. To ensure his own authority in the country, Carrillo also took Costa Rica out of the United Provinces of Central America.

Prospering coffee planters, who opposed the control and taxation of their businesses by the central government, resisted Carrillo. To aid their cause, coffee growers and other landowners enlisted the help of General Francisco Morazán Quesada, former president of the United Provinces. Morazán arrived in Costa Rica in April 1842 with an army of volunteer soldiers. Carrillo's own forces revolted against Carrillo and went over to Morazán's side.

Carrillo fled to El Salvador, and Morazán was named the provisional president of Costa Rica. But when Morazán tried to revive the United Provinces of Central America, which had disbanded in 1838, he faced a public uprising from Costa Ricans who did not want their country to lose its independence. Morazán fled but was captured in Cartago and brought back to San José, where he was executed.

Costa Rica and the other small republics of Central America made a tempting target for foreign conquerors. In the 1850s, U.S. adventurer William Walker invaded Central America from the north and took over Nicaragua. Walker's campaign to conquer and rule Central America had the support of many U.S. governement and business leaders, including

William Walker's men, called *filibusteros*, fight during the Battle of Rivas. Costa Rican volunteers pushed Walker's men out of Costa Rica and to Rivas, Nicaragua, defeating them there on April 11, 1856. Walker then fled Latin America.

Cornelius Vanderbilt, a rich businessman with extensive Central American investments. But Walker and his army of mercenaries (hired soldiers) ran into strong resistance, put up by an army of Costa Rican volunteers led by Juan Rafael Mora. The Costa Ricans defeated Walker's troops in 1856, a victory that brought a new sense of nationhood and common interest to the various towns and regions of Costa Rica.

## A New Constitution

Costa Rican voters elected General Togas Guardia as president in 1870. Guardia's administration built new schools and roads, largely through taxes levied on wealthy landowners. Guardia also spearheaded construction of the Atlantic Railway, stretching from the Atlantic coast to San José. The railway provided a cheap and fast way to transport Costa Rica's coffee, which producers previously had to ship from the Pacific to the Atlantic by sending it around Cape Horn, at the tip of South America. The railway also encouraged investment by U.S. companies, including United Fruit, which opened banana plantations on Costa Rica's Caribbean coast. Economic opportunities also attracted immigrants from foreign countries, including China, Great Britain, and Germany, as well as other regions of Latin America.

## MINOR KEITH'S GOOD DEAL

The construction of the Atlantic Railway from San José to the Caribbean coast was proving difficult and expensive. The railroad had first been planned by Henry Meiggs, a U.S. businessman in Costa Rica. But it was Meiggs's nephew, Minor Cooper Keith, who carried out the project.

A wealthy banana planter, Keith had made his fortune planting banana trees in the clearings made by his uncle's company for the railroad. Seeing another opportunity in the unfinished railway, Keith struck a deal with the Costa Rican government in 1883. In return for completing the railroad, he was given land—a total of 7 percent of all the land in Costa Rica. After seven years of grueling work, the railroad was finally completed in 1890.

Thanks to Keith's railroad, Costa Rica's banana industry flourished for several decades. The railway moved the perishable (easily spoiled) bananas quickly from plantations to the coast, where they were shipped to markets in the United States. Bananas soon surpassed coffee as the most important Costa Rican export.

After Guardia's death in 1882, a new generation of leaders emerged, determined to follow through on the reforms of the Guardia presidency. In 1889 Costa Rica drafted a new constitution, which established regular elections to take place every four years. All men of European descent were allowed to vote, but women, blacks, and Indians still did not have this right.

By then the coffee industry formed the backbone of the Costa Rican economy. Thousands of small, independent landowners produced coffee beans, which were sold to processing facilities located on much larger properties. The wealthy coffee processors made up a powerful oligarchy—an economic and political elite—which dominated the Costa Rican government. Through the late nineteenth and early twentieth centuries, Costa Rican presidents found they could not rule without the support of this elite.

**Workers cut bananas** bound for U.S. markets via the Atlantic Railway in the early 1900s.

Visit www.vgsbooks.com for links to websites with additional information about the Costa Rican government and history, including the Battle of Rivas, national hero Juan Santamaría, and Costa Rica's civil war of 1948.

In the meantime, more foreign companies arrived to take advantage of cheap land and low labor costs in Costa Rica. Bananas, mostly grown on U.S.-owned plantations, became a key export. But foreign trade slowed with the outbreak of World War I in 1914. Merchant ships were unable to risk travel on the high seas, where submarines and battleships were stopping and sinking cargo vessels. To make up for the loss of income from taxes on exports, President Alfredo González Flores began levying a tax directly on coffee planters. Strongly opposed to this measure, the planters supported Federico Tinoco Granados, the minister of war, in a coup that took place on January 27, 1917.

Tinoco established a dictatorship—a government in which he wielded sole and oppressive power. But an uprising by workers and the poor in San José brought down the Tinoco government in 1919. Social reformers, who favored the redistribution of land from wealthy landowners to rural laborers, were becoming popular. In 1923 the Reformist Party formed to promote these goals.

More radical than the Reformist Party, a Communist Party formed in Costa Rica in 1931. The Communist ideology, based on state control of the economy with no private property, found a wide audience among Costa Rican workers, many of whom labored with little hope of ever owning property or gaining a measure of economic independence. Communism gained further support during the worldwide economic depression of the early 1930s, when exports fell along with wages in Costa Rica and unemployment rose sharply.

In the countryside as well as the city, working conditions were poor for many. Banana workers, for example, labored on disease-infested plantations for wages that barely kept their families fed. These conditions made the Caribbean "banana coast" a fertile ground for labor organizers. In 1934 the Communist Party led a huge strike by banana workers, who found the Costa Rican government taking their side in a dispute with their employer, the U.S.-based United Fruit Company. The company agreed to some of the workers' demands, including equal pay for black workers. But United Fruit soon moved its plantations to a remote stretch of coastal lowlands along the Pacific Ocean, where it could operate independently of government supervision and thus avoid giving more rights to workers.

In 1940 Dr. Rafael Angel Calderón Guardia won the presidency with 85 percent of the vote. During his presidency, Calderón brought about important reforms. His government enacted a minimum-wage law, granted benefits to disabled workers, set up a social security system, and passed new labor laws that gave workers the right to organize and strike. These new laws angered coffee planters. In need of allies, the president formed an alliance with the Catholic Church and the Communist Party.

One of Calderón's followers, Teodoro Picado Michalski, was elected to the presidency in 1944. But Picado faced strong opposition from Calderón's enemies, who claimed electoral fraud. A series of strikes and demonstrations in 1947 further divided Costa Rican society.

## The Figueres Government

In 1948 Calderón again ran for president. His opponent, Otilio Ulate Blanco, claimed victory, but this time Calderón charged election fraud, and the legislature declared the election void. Fearful of Calderón's Communist ties, a landowner named José "Pepe" Figueres Ferrer emerged as a leader of the Calderón opposition. In a conflict known as the War of National Liberation, Figueres took up arms against Calderón's supporters. The war lasted forty-four days and resulted in

**Calderón supporters, called *mariachis*, march into battle** during the Costa Rican civil war of 1948. Calderón's forces ultimately lost to opposition forces, and Calderón left office.

**José "Pepe" Figueres** *(standing at left in black suit)* and supporters celebrate their victory over Calderón's forces. The victory paved the way for Figueres to take over the Costa Rican government in 1948.

the deaths of two thousand Costa Ricans. Figueres's forces triumphed, and Figueres became interim president of Costa Rica.

Figueres established what he called the Second Republic of Costa Rica. Although fiercely anti-Communist, he also proved to be a reformer. He levied new taxes on the wealthy, raised the minimum wage for workers, and seized private banks, turning them over to the government. A new constitution of 1949 reflected Figueres's goals and ideals, including strict regulation and supervision of private property, such as large farms and businesses. The constitution also granted citizenship and voting rights to everyone born in Costa Rica (except indigenous people). Figueres abolished the Costa Rican army, which he saw as an unnecessary public expense. Military facilities became schools, prisons, and other public institutions. Figueres also limited the terms of high-level police officials, preventing them from growing too powerful. In another important reform, the Figueres government established a Supreme Tribunal, whose job was to oversee presidential elections and ensure their fairness.

Figueres served as president from 1953 to 1957 and again from 1970 to 1974. His National Liberation Party (the initials of its Spanish name—Partido Liberación Nacional—are PLN) became one of the two major political parties of Costa Rica. Although he was not always in power, Figueres inspired many new social programs and reforms carried out in the last half of the twentieth century. Without an army to support, the government turned much of its budget toward education, health care, and workers' benefits.

In the meantime, a rising international demand for Costa Rican exports, particularly coffee, bananas, and cacao (cocoa beans, from which chocolate is made), brought about an improving economy. A strong middle class of merchants and rural landowners arose. This middle class was largely supportive of the government reforms and the democratic electoral process. These trends brought Costa Rica much envied stability at a time when many Latin American nations were undergoing bitter civil conflict between haves and have-nots.

## An Economic Crisis

In the 1970s, Costa Rica entered a severe economic downturn. In part, the problems were brought about by the country's success. Confident of continued growth, the government had borrowed money from foreign banks to invest in business development. An Arab oil embargo (prohibition on trade) in the 1970s, however, caused steep rises in the cost of energy, which in turn touched off economic inflation. At the same time, escalating warfare in neighboring Nicaragua made Costa Rica less attractive to foreign investment. Costa Rica found itself with a budget deficit (shortfall), a currency losing its value, and debts it couldn't pay. By the early 1980s, poverty was increasing, and inflation was spiraling out of control.

In need of help, Costa Rica turned to the World Bank, an international lending agency. In return for low-interest loans, the World Bank implemented new economic policies in Costa Rica. To balance its budget, Costa Rica had to cut public spending and privatize state-held companies—that is, sell them to private investors. This action aroused controversy and opposition among voters, as many Costa Ricans strongly favored state ownership of vital industries and resources.

In 1986 Oscar Arias Sánchez of the PLN won the presidential election. Arias left his mark in foreign affairs by helping end civil wars in El Salvador and Nicaragua and creating a largely successful peace plan for all of Central America. For his efforts, Arias was awarded the Nobel Peace Prize in 1987.

In 1994 José María Figueres Olsen, the son of José Figueres Ferrer, won the presidency, also as a PLN candidate. The son could not match his father's popularity, however, and found himself battling economic problems and rising civil unrest.

In 1998 Miguel Ángel Rodriguez Echeverría of the Social Christian Unity Party (the initials of its Spanish name are PUSC) was elected president. Although the economy improved under Rodriguez, many Costa Ricans strongly opposed his attempt to further privatize state-held companies. Rodriguez also found himself contending with another economic downturn late in his term.

**Abel Pacheco greets supporters in Cartago, Costa Rica,** following the 2002 election. Receiving 58 percent of the vote, Pacheco secured the presidency during an election runoff. It was the first runoff in Costa Rican history.

In 2002 a third-party candidate, Ottón Solís of the Citizen Action Party, gained widespread support. But by then, many voters had lost faith and interest in the electoral process. With about 30 percent of voters failing to cast ballots, neither the PUSC nor the PLN won the 40 percent of the votes needed to win the 2002 election. In the runoff that followed in April, PUSC's Abel Pacheco won—this time with nearly 40 percent of voters staying home. A television commentator and writer, well known to the Costa Rican public, Pacheco promised an inclusive government that would listen to all sides of disputes and issues. Taking a conservative line on public spending, Pacheco also pledged to slim down government bureaucracy and reduce wasteful spending.

In the first years of the 2000s, Costa Rica wanted to expand its trade with the United States. In early 2004, after several years of negotiation, Costa Rica signed the Central American Free Trade Agreement, or CAFTA. CAFTA members can export goods to the rest of Central America and to the United States without paying duties (taxes) on them. In addition, CAFTA will bring more foreign business, in search of low-cost labor, to Central America.

Through its history, Costa Rica has written several constitutions, each of which has set out a new form of government and principles that would guide the country's judicial, legislative, and executive branches. Different constitutions were created in 1821, 1824, 1825, 1844, 1871, and 1949. The 1949 constitution is still in force. To learn more, visit www.vgsbooks.com.

## ⊙ Government

Costa Rica is a democratic republic—a state in which voters elect representatives to govern on their behalf. The president, elected for a four-year term, is the head of government and head of state. The government also has two vice presidents and a twelve-member cabinet (cabinet members head government departments such as the Ministry of Finance, Ministry of Education, and so on).

The Legislative Assembly, or congress, includes fifty-seven deputies who serve four-year terms. The assembly makes laws for the nation. Neither the president nor the deputies can serve more than one term back-to-back.

The Legislative Assembly appoints the twenty-two justices of Costa Rica's supreme court, who serve eight-year terms. Supreme court judges select lower court judges. A Supreme Tribunal, consisting of three judges, oversees elections to guarantee their fairness and the right of all Costa Rican citizens to vote (Indians finally won that right in 1991).

**A Costa Rican nun leaves a voting station** after casting her ballot during the 2002 presidential election. To help ease fears created from Costa Rica's once stormy political system, a sign promises voters that their votes are secret.

Voting is required for all citizens eighteen years and older, although the percentage of citizens who actually vote declined in the late twentieth century. A voter's registration card serves as a national identity card, and all Costa Ricans are required to carry one. Two major parties—the National Liberation Party and the Social Christian Unity Party—have shared political power over the last fifty years.

Costa Rica is divided into seven provinces: San José, Alajuela, Cartago, Heredia, Guanacaste, Puntarenas, and Limón. The president appoints the governors of these provinces. The country is further divided into eighty-one counties and 429 districts, which handle matters of local governance. Elected officials govern at the local level.

# THE PEOPLE

Costa Rica's population is 3.9 million people. The population is growing at the rate of 1.7 percent a year, bringing a projected population of 5.2 million in the year 2025. The overall population density (number of people living on a certain amount of land) is 200 people per square mile (77 people per sq. km), somewhat higher than the rest of Central America, which has a density of 146 people per square mile (56 people per sq. km).

Despite population pressures, Costa Rica enjoys a high standard of living, good overall health care and educational systems, and political stability. Although a variety of ethnic groups make up Costa Rican society, the country has largely avoided the tension among ethnic groups and social classes that besets many other Latin American nations.

## Ethnic Groups

The indigenous peoples of Costa Rica numbered about 400,000 when Europeans first began settling the region during the sixteenth century.

With the arrival of Europeans, the indigenous population quickly declined. Many Indians died of diseases brought by the Europeans. Others were killed in warfare. By the beginning of the twenty-first century, indigenous people numbered only about 15,000, or less than 1 percent of the Costa Rican population.

The largest remaining indigenous groups are the Bribrí, the Cabecares, the Borucas, and the Guayamís. Most indigenous families live in Limón Province, but many, such as the Bribrí, still live in the remote Talamanca Range. The Bribrí still practice their traditional religion. Their shamans practice and teach traditional medicine. They invoke the spirits of healing gods in songs and chants and use "healing sticks," etched with pictures of healing gods, a patient's illness, and the plants used to cure it. The Guaymí Indians, who live in southern Costa Rica near Panama, make beaded necklaces known as *chaquiras.* Formerly worn by warriors, chaquiras are sold to tourists in modern times.

## A DECADE OF VICTORIES

The indigenous peoples of Costa Rica have seen their cultures and languages largely disappear over the five centuries since Christopher Columbus arrived in Central America. But finally, in the 1990s, Costa Rican Indians won several important victories. In 1991 the Costa Rican legislature officially granted Indians full citizenship and the right to vote. In 1992 the government signed the United Nations Treaty on Indigenous Populations and Tribes. With this treaty, Indians won the right to bilingual education (instruction in both Spanish and indigenous languages), as well as full sovereignty (political control) over the country's twenty-two indigenous reserves. In 1995 a Spanish-Bribrí language high school, the nation's first bilingual school, opened in the Talamanca region.

Costa Rica has twenty-two indigenous reserves, or reservations, areas set aside for use by native peoples. The government first set up the reserves in 1971 and banned any settlement or development by nonindigenous people there. Despite the law, non-Indians have invaded several reserves, clearing the land for live-stock and crops and prospecting for minerals.

For three centuries after the arrival of Europeans, immigrants from Spain and Spain's other American colonies dominated Costa Rican society. These criollos, people of purely European ancestry, made up Costa Rica's governing, landowning, and merchant classes. Some of these newcomers inter-married with indigenous peoples and had children, creating a mestizo class. People of European descent, including mestizos, make up about 94 percent of Costa Rica's total population.

In many Latin American coun-tries, vast class differences devel-oped between criollos, mestizos, and indigenous people. However, Costa Rica's isolation and limited

**A Bribrí Indian family** swims in a reserve river. In 1992 the Bribrí and other native peoples of Costa Rica won the right to control reserve lands set aside for them. For more information about Costa Rica's native peoples, visit www.vgsbooks.com.

**Costa Ricans with criollo and mestizo heritage** on a busy street in San José. Most Costa Ricans are of criollo and mestizo descent. For links to information about the people of Costa Rica, visit www.vgsbooks.com.

economy brought about a leveling of society. Because trade was limited and manufacturing nearly nonexistent, there was little difference between rich and poor. Everyone had to work the land to survive.

Costa Rica received an influx of new immigrants in the late nineteenth century. These newcomers included English and German immigrants who sought economic opportunities, either as workers or landowners, in Costa Rica's prospering coffee industry. They spread through the country with the help of the new Atlantic Railway linking the cities of the Central Valley to Puerto Limón. The railroad, in turn, hired Chinese and Italian immigrants, who later took other jobs in the nation's growing cities. These groups formed distinct ethnic communities. Once established and successful, they sponsored the arrival of family members from abroad, who also began to climb the economic ladder.

Costa Ricans of Chinese heritage are known as Chinos. Their immigration to Costa Rica began in 1855, when Costa Rica needed laborers to help construct new railways. After starting out as railroad workers, many Chinos became merchants and shopkeepers in San José and other major cities. The latest Chinese immigrants in Costa Rica come from Hong Kong, once a British-controlled colony that reverted to control by mainland China in 1997. In modern times, Chinos comprise less than 1 percent of the nation's overall population.

## ACHIEVING EQUALITY

Through the early twentieth century, black Costa Ricans were not considered citizens of the country where they were born and lived. They could not own land or move about the country freely. The situation changed when José Figueres took power after the 1948 civil war. Figueres granted black Costa Ricans full citizenship, although Indians didn't win citizenship rights until many years later. Find links to more information about human rights in Costa Rica at www.vgsbooks.com.

Black Costa Ricans, living mainly in Puerto Limón and along the eastern coast, make up about 2 percent of the population. They descend primarily from African slaves, brought to Costa Rica in the early years of Spanish colonization, and Afro-Caribbean settlers, who arrived from Jamaica and other islands to work on banana plantations or the Atlantic Railway. For many years, the Costa Rican government denied blacks citizenship and the right to vote. The constitution of 1949 finally gave Afro-Costa Ricans equal rights, however. Many Jamaican-descended Costa Ricans maintain a distinct culture from other Costa Ricans. Instead of Spanish, they speak English as their first language. The remaining 2 percent of Costa Rica's population is made up of people with a variety backgrounds, including Asians and Middle Easterners.

In the twentieth century, French, Germans, British, Italians, and North Americans settled in as well, some of them marrying Costa Ricans. Costa Rican prosperity and stability have also attracted immigrants from South America. Many North Americans and Europeans have retired in Costa Rica. The nation's lax business regulations have encouraged the establishment of small "offshore" companies, foreign-owned businesses operating in Costa Rica.

## Education

Costa Ricans take pride in their system of public education, which originated during the 1820s, immediately after independence. In 1869 education became free and mandatory for all Costa Rican citizens. The sweeping reforms that began in the late 1940s focused largely on the educational system. The government devoted a large portion of its budget to building and maintaining new schools. Teachers earned good pay and retirement benefits, and schools were built in remote rural areas.

In modern times, about 20 percent of the national budget goes to education. Costa Rica requires school attendance for children ages six to fourteen, and schooling is free through the twelfth grade.

Ninety-five percent of Costa Ricans are literate, the highest literacy rate in Latin America.

The school year in Costa Rica runs from February to October, with a three-month break beginning in November (traditionally, the break allowed students to help with the all-important coffee harvest). After nine years of primary schooling, students may enter the workforce or continue on to high school, where they can choose from either a job-training or an academic program. To graduate, high school (and university) students must complete a program of community service, which involves working in poor neighborhoods as teachers, health aides, or manual laborers.

The first institution of higher learning in Costa Rica was the University of Santo Tomas, founded in San José in 1843. The modern successor to this school is the University of Costa Rica, a public school established in 1940. A public technical institute, where students train for fields such as engineering, architecture, and computer programming, operates in Cartago. The public State University at a Distance allows students in isolated regions to take correspondence courses, communicating with teachers via mail or the Internet. Private universities, concentrated in the capital, also operate in Costa Rica. Costa Rica's universities draw students from several other Latin American nations. The medical school at the University of Costa Rica enjoys a reputation as the finest in Central America.

**Costa Rican schoolchildren** take a break between classes. In 1869 Costa Rica became one of the first countries in the world to provide free, mandatory education to its citizens.

The Costa Rican educational system is not free of problems and controversy, however. Many young Costa Ricans drop out of school before age fourteen in order to work and help support their families. In the late 1990s, about 92 percent of primary-school-age children (age fourteen and under) attended school, while only about 55 percent of high-school-age children did so. In recent years, budget cutbacks have brought cuts in teacher salaries and left many schools poorly funded. Schools have shortages of books and basic equipment such as desks, paper, and chalkboards. Many teachers are not trained or certified by the state. Over the years, local school systems have shortened the school year and school day to save money.

## Health and Welfare

The 1949 constitution placed a strong emphasis on health care and social welfare. In 1970 the government created a new agency, the Social Assistance Institute, to provide basic health care and social welfare programs to all citizens. Medical care was nationalized, or taken over by the government. The government made sure that people in poor rural areas received medical care and utilities such as clean water. The government also set up vaccination programs to protect the young and elderly from diseases and set up welfare programs, job-training programs, and a social security system. After these programs were created, poverty, disease, and infant death rates fell dramatically.

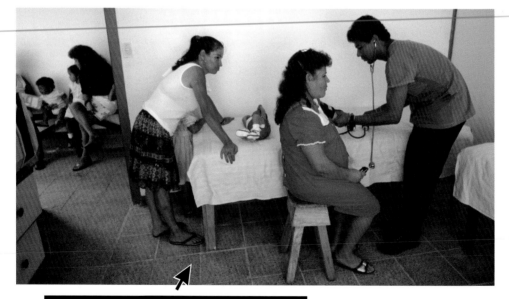

**Women and children receive medical checkups** at a rural Costa Rican clinic. Clinics such as this one have helped fight disease and prevent unnecessary deaths in Costa Rica. If you'd like to learn more about Costa Rica's health and education systems, visit www.vgsbooks.com for links.

The economic crisis of the 1970s lowered state spending on social welfare programs, however. Yet through the 1980s and 1990s, Costa Rica continued to fight poverty, poor housing, and a lack of education among its citizens. The government targeted its efforts at certain poor districts. It helped families pay for rent, school expenses, and food. These efforts have proved successful. In the early 2000s, about 95 percent of Costa Rican neighborhoods have clean drinking water, electricity, and basic sanitation services.

The country spends about 7 percent of its income on health services. It has about 1.4 doctors for every 1,000 people, a good percentage within Central America. Life expectancy averages 77 years (75 years for men and 79 years for women), the best rates in Central America. Infant mortality (death rates) stands at 11 deaths per 1,000 births, the lowest rate in the region.

The typical Costa Rican woman will have 2.7 children in her lifetime. About 80 percent of women between the ages of 15 and 49 use birth control, the highest percentage in Central America. Nevertheless, the incidence of teen pregnancy rose steadily in the 1990s, particularly in rural areas. In 1998 the government started two educational programs, Young Love and Constructing Opportunities, aimed at teaching Costa Rican teenagers about human sexuality, pregnancy, and parenting.

The generally high standard of living in Costa Rica, compared with its Central American neighbors, means a lower rate of homelessness and fewer destitute people on the streets. However, Costa Rica still struggles with a number of social problems. Drug abuse is growing, particularly in San José and other large cities, where juveniles and young adults have access to illegal drugs such as cocaine. The drug problem is linked to a low but growing crime problem in the cities, home to well-organized criminal gangs. The number of Costa Ricans living with HIV (the human immunodeficiency virus, the virus that causes acquired immune difficiency syndrome, or AIDS) reached about 11,000 in the early 2000s, a low number in Central America.

# CULTURAL LIFE

Costa Ricans take great pride in their country's lively and unique culture. The country has produced renowned writers, artists, musicians, and other performers. After passage of the 1949 constitution, the government took on a new role in fostering the arts. It began to provide funding for national theater, music, and arts organizations. The Ministry of Culture sponsors musical and theatrical productions throughout the country. Costa Rica also hosts many musical stars from throughout Latin America and puts on lively music and arts festivals throughout the year.

## Language and Literature

The indigenous languages of Costa Rica include Maleku, Bribrí, Guaymí, Cabecar, and Brunca. Early indigenous tribes had no written language. They passed down their history and traditions through folktales and songs, many of which are still told and sung to younger generations. Over centuries of Spanish settlement and domination, most of Costa Rica's indigenous languages died out. However, in recent decades,

Costa Ricans have made efforts to revive and protect some indigenous languages. In the twenty-first century, some indigenous communities broadcast news and other programs over indigenous-language radio stations such as Radio Maleku and Voice of Talamanca.

Spanish arrived with the explorers of the early sixteenth century, and it served as the principal language of the Costa Rican colonists. It later became—and remains—the official language of Costa Rica.

In the nineteenth century, Costa Rican writers began creating essays known as *cuadros,* short but realistic portrayals of everyday life. Most cuadros described poor farmers or laboring families, struggling to survive and prosper in harsh circumstances. The *cuadro* and the related style of *costumbrismo* reached the height of their popularity in the late nineteenth century. Many *cuadros* appeared in Sunday newspapers, where they gained a national audience.

Carmen Lyra was a famous Costa Rican writer of the early twentieth century. *Tales of My Aunt Panchita,* written in 1920, remains her

## NAME GAME

In Costa Rica and other Spanish-speaking countries, many people take the last names of both their mothers and their fathers. For example, Oscar Arias Sánchez's name comes from his father's last name—Arias—plus his mother's last name—Sánchez. The father's name comes first and cannot be left out. For instance, you might see him referred to as Oscar Arias or Oscar Arias Sánchez, but never as Oscar Sánchez. Not all Spanish names follow this rule, however, a fact that can lead to confusion for non-Spanish-speaking people.

most famous work. Lyra also wrote *Christmas Fantasy,* a well-known children's play. Two of her books, *Bananas and Men* and *Golden Bean,* took a hard look at Costa Rica's social and economic injustices.

A leader of the 1934 banana workers' strike against the United Fruit Company, Carlos Luis Fallas wrote in a style called social realism, a genre that attempts to depict everyday life, stripped of artistic literary effects. His *Mamita Yunai* is a fictional account of the struggles of banana workers. The book inspired similar works by writers in the neighboring countries of Honduras and Panama, where working conditions on banana plantations were no better.

Costa Rica's best-known author, Carmen Naranjo, was nominated for a Nobel Prize for Literature in 1998. Born in 1928, she has served her country as minister of culture and ambassador to Israel. In her novels and short stories, such as *There Never Was a Once Upon a Time,* Naranjo often addresses current issues and trends, such as Costa Rica's rapid modernization and lost traditions. Her works have been translated into English and several other languages. She is the only Costa Rican author to be widely read outside of the country.

## ◉ Music

Costa Rica's musical traditions date back thousands of years, to the percussion and wind instruments fashioned by the country's indigenous peoples. Traditional instruments included flutes made of animal bones, maracas (bean-filled gourds), and drums made of animal skins. The *quijongo* resembled a guitar. It had a single string, a wooden neck, and a sound box made from a hollow gourd. The marimba, a percussion instrument, was made from a series of hollow gourds and wooden keys and was struck with sticks or mallets. Costa Rican musicians still use modern versions of many traditional instruments.

Guanacaste Province is famous for its traditional music, performed with marimbas and guitars. Many songwriters from this region have

**Street musicians perform traditional Costa Rican music** with guitars and an accordion. Spaniards introduced the guitar and the accordion to Costa Rica when Spaniards began to settle the country.

created ballads celebrating daily life and the beauty of nature. The songs of Guanacaste have found an audience throughout Central America and in more distant countries.

On the opposite coast, Limón Province claims its own, very distinct musical heritage. Musical styles such as calypso and reggae, imported from the islands of the Caribbean, can be heard throughout the day, on the streets and on the radio. At the Limón Carnival in October, musicians and dancers perform a lilting calypso style. In February the Monteverde Music Festival, held at the Monteverde Cloud Forest Preserve, presents classical, jazz, and folk music. The same month, Puerto Viejo de Talamanca holds a festival of Caribbean music.

San José hosts the National Symphony Orchestra, the National Chorus, and an annual opera performance. In the capital's nightclubs, dozens of groups perform salsa and merengue rhythms (both Caribbean styles), enjoyed by dancing patrons. Much of the popular music in Costa Rica blends such Latin styles with rock and pop music imported from North America.

## Film, Theater, and Media

Costa Rican cinema originated in the 1930s with *El Retorno (The Return),* a fictional film by director A. F. Bertoni. For many years afterward, however, moviemaking came under harsh criticism by the Catholic Church, which viewed fictional movies as dangerous and immoral. So most Costa Rican films treated nonfiction documentary subjects, such as the nation's elections or economic development.

In the 1970s, a strong movie industry began to develop, however. Since that time, the Costa Rican Center of Cinematographic Production in San José has supported directors, film editors, and actors. San José also stages an annual Contest of Cinema and Video. Costa Rica's striking volcanoes, mountain ranges, and rain forests have also provided a backdrop for hundreds of feature-length movies, including the U.S.-made films *Congo* (1995) and *The Blue Butterfly* (2002).

**According to Costa Rican tradition, the Teatro Nacional, or National Theater, resulted from an opera singer's tantrum. It is said that the famous Spanish singer Adelina Patti refused to perform in San José, complaining that the stages were not suitable. In response, Costa Rican coffee growers placed a tax on each bag of coffee beans that left the country. With the money from the tax, Costa Rica was able to build the Teatro Nacional in downtown San José. It became the premier stage for music and theater in all of Central America. For infomation links, visit www.vgsbooks.com.**

San José, the site of the first stages and movie theaters in Costa Rica, has become a Central American capital for theater. The National Theater, built in the 1890s, stages a concert, an opera, a ballet, or a play nearly every night of the week. Actors also perform plays on outdoor plazas, allowing large audiences to gather informally. Each year, San José hosts an arts festival featuring foreign and native music and theater groups, as well as dozens of gallery showings for the country's leading artists.

Costa Rica features a lively news media, which enjoys the principle of press freedom written into the 1949 constitution. Three national newspapers—*La Nación,* the oldest and largest paper, *La Republica,* and *La Prensa Libre*—appear daily. These papers compete with weekly and monthly journals covering news, fashion, entertainment, and sports. The *Tico Times,* published weekly in San José, is the leading English-language newspaper in Central America.

Television arrived in the 1950s. By the start of the twenty-first century, more than 90 percent of Costa Rican households owned at least one television set. The government runs one TV station, while more than a dozen private, commercial stations also operate. Cable systems bring a wide array of programming from Latin America and the United States. An evening news program, *Telenoticias,* has a national audience. Costa Rican stations also broadcast soap operas, game shows, variety shows, and sports.

A Costa Rican man reads a newspaper outside a Point Quepos **information café.** In addition to serving coffee and tapas (light meals), the café offers customers newspapers, books, and Internet access. Visit www.vgsbooks.com for a link to the Costa Rican newspaper the *Tico Times* and for links to information about Costa Rica's arts and culture.

Nearly everyone in Costa Rica listens to music, sports, talk shows, soap operas, and news broadcasts on the radio. Transistor radios in isolated villages provide residents with a link to the capital city and current events on the national and international scene.

Cyber-cafés in San José and other cities offer access to the Internet. E-mail and chat rooms have become popular ways for Costa Ricans to communicate with each other and with friends in foreign countries. Cell phones still represent an expensive luxury for most Costa Ricans. About one million households have regular phone service, while about half as many have personal computers in the home.

## Art and Architecture

Skilled in working wood and stone, the early indigenous tribes of Costa Rica created a wide variety of useful craft objects, including pottery, basketry, textiles, jewelry, and clothing. Many of these items are still made, both for everyday use and for sale to tourists. The Chorotegas still build clay jugs and bowls by hand, without potter's wheels, and paint these items with a mixture of water, sand, and clay. The Boruca Indians use balsa and cedar wood to make elaborate masks. The masks are used in an annual festival, the Dance of the Little Devils, which celebrates the struggle of the Indians against the colonization of Central America by the Spanish.

The costumbrismo style of writing has its counterpart in works of visual art that depict everyday life in rural Costa Rica. For instance, the paintings of Teodorico Quiros (1897–1977) celebrate simple yet colorful scenes of the countryside. (Quiros also worked as an architect and designed many churches and public buildings in Costa Rica.) In the mid-twentieth century, many Costa Rican artists left behind traditional styles to create abstract works, which did not show recognizable people or places.

Sculptures in stone and bronze adorn many public parks and streets, particularly in the capital. Francisco Zuñiga (1912–1998), one of the most famous Latin American artists of the twentieth century, has left characteristic works all over the urban landscape of Costa Rica. Zuñiga learned techniques of stone sculpture and metalworking in Mexico City, where he made his home. He is best known for his female figures, rounded and massive, depicted in painting, prints, and stone sculpture.

Early indigenous Costa Ricans built homes and other structures out of stone. The remains of ancient stone houses, terraces, walkways and aqueducts can still be seen at Guayabo National Monument in Cartago Province. Many modern homes in Costa Rica are built in the Spanish colonial style. This style features smooth stone walls covered

Many Costa Ricans live in Spanish colonial-style homes. This shopping center is built in the same style but with more detail, such as columns.

with whitewash and beamed roofs covered by rows of interlocking clay tiles. Many homes stand close to the street in front, with small private gardens or yards to the rear. More elaborate homes are surrounded by stone walls for privacy.

Many public buildings, especially from the colonial era, were built in a monumental neoclassical style, which features tall columns, massive facades (fronts), tall windows, and grand outer staircases. Many of these features were borrowed from popular European architecture of the late nineteenth and early twentieth centuries. In the cities, buildings are often constructed around large plazas. The plazas serve as a site for markets, festivals, and celebrations. Many people take evening walks on the plazas, where they like to talk and exchange news.

## ◐ Religion

The vast majority of Costa Ricans are Roman Catholic, and the Roman Catholic Church has played an important role in the country's history. Spanish rulers, conquistadors (conquerors), and early settlers all wanted to convert native peoples to Christianity, specifically Catholicism. The Spanish built churches in Costa Rica, forced indigenous people to convert to Catholicism, and established missions, or estates where church leaders taught the faith and converted nonbelievers to the faith. Cartago was the site of the first two Catholic cathedrals in Costa Rica.

As Catholicism spread, indigenous religion began to die out. By the middle of the nineteenth century, it was practiced only in isolated indigenous villages. In 1852 Catholicism became the official religion of Costa Rica.

In the twenty-first century, about nine out of ten Costa Ricans claim membership in the Roman Catholic Church, although a much smaller percentage actually attend Mass regularly. Every Catholic child is baptized into the Church and takes first Communion

### A PATRON SAINT

The patron saint of Costa Rica, the Virgin of the Angels, is known as La Negrita, "the dark-skinned one." This saint is said to have appeared on top of a rock in the town of Cartago in 1635. The Basilica of Our Lady of the Angels was built on that site. A nearby stream is said to carry water with miraculous healing powers. Glass cases within the underground chambers of the cathedral hold hundreds of small clay charms, in the shape of arms, legs, and feet, representing limbs believed to have been healed by these holy waters. An annual 14-mile (22.5-km) pilgrimage known as La Romería takes place in August. On this walk, the faithful travel from San José to Cartago. The pilgrimage ends with a feast in honor of the patron saint.

at age eight or nine. Most people observe Catholic holidays, particularly Holy Week, which ends on Easter Sunday.

Despite the dominance of the Catholic Church, Protestants (non-Catholic Christians) are present in growing numbers in Costa Rica. Protestant missionaries, teachers who seek to convert others to their beliefs and churches, have been arriving in Costa Rica from the United States since the early twentieth century. Protestant Costa Ricans include Baptists, Methodists, Mormons, and Jehovah's Witnesses.

On the Caribbean coast, black Costa Ricans, many of whom trace their ancestry to Jamaica, belong to the Baptist and Anglican churches, which were also attended by English-speaking settlers in the Caribbean Islands. Certain religious practices that originated in Africa also survive among black Costa Ricans. For instance, the rites of West Indian Obeahism, in which a shaman summons good and evil spirits, have blended with Christian holidays and observances, particularly in Puerto Limón and the surrounding region.

Jews, who claim about 1 percent of the total population, make up a small community in several large Costa Rican towns. Many Jews arrived from Eastern Europe in the years before and after World War II (1939–1945) as refugees from the war and from persecution by Germany's Nazi government.

Despite the dominance of Catholicism, the indigenous people of Costa Rica have preserved many rituals and traditions of their religious faith, in which sacred sites and animals are considered to hold supernatural powers. In some surviving tribes, shamans still heal the sick and injured with prayers, music, and medicinal plants. The Bribrí Indians have retained some elaborate funeral traditions. The Bribrí believe the soul of a dead person goes through several incarnations (rebirths), according to a person's behavior on earth, before finding its final resting place.

## Holidays and Festivals

The Costa Rican calendar includes both public and religious holidays. Saint Joseph's Day, March 19, honors the patron saint of the capital city of San José. April 11 is Juan Santamaría Day, who gave his life setting fire to the stronghold of William Walker's filibusteros during the Battle of Rivas. Alajuela, Santamaría's hometown, hosts parades and other special events on this day.

May 1 is Labor Day, a holiday that honors the country's workers. July 25 is the Day of Guanacaste, which observes the 1825 annexation of Guanacaste Province, which had once been part of Nicaragua. On August 15, Costa Ricans celebrate Mother's Day. September 15 is the nation's Independence Day, when Costa Ricans celebrate the freedom won from Spain in 1821. On October 12, Día de la Raza (Day of the

**A Costa Rican dancer** stops to display her dress during an event celebrating Afro-Caribbean history and culture in Puerto Limón.

People) celebrates the arrival of Europeans in Latin America. (While this honoring of Christopher Columbus and other explorers is an old tradition in Costa Rica, in recent years debate has flared over European colonization, which destroyed many of Costa Rica's indigenous groups.)

Holy Week, the week before Easter, is a time of traditional church celebrations. As in many Catholic countries, the Thursday and Friday before Easter Sunday (Holy Thursday and Good Friday) are national holidays. On August 2, the Virgin of the Angels is honored with a national holiday. On this day, pilgrims walk along the road from San José to Cartago. Christmas Day, December 25, is also a national holiday. A week of celebrations, including dances, parades, and religious observance, ends with a national party on New Year's Eve.

## Sports

Soccer is nearly everywhere in Costa Rica. Even the smallest towns and villages have soccer fields, which remain busy almost all year long. The national professional soccer league, the Costa Rican Football Federation, holds its championship matches in the early summer.

The nation's business comes to a halt during important international matches. Costa Rica's appearance among the teams competing for the 2002 World Cup remains a national point of pride, as does an appearance in the quarterfinals of the 1990 World Cup.

Many Costa Ricans have a passion for exercise and fitness. Walkers, joggers, and bicyclists crowd the city streets. Those with the means join private health clubs, while many more join basketball, volleyball, baseball, and soccer teams. Children play soccer, tag, hide-and-seek, and other games in open spaces and city parks.

Costa Rica's landscape attracts outdoor sports enthusiasts from all over the world. Surfers ride the breaking waves along the 600-mile (965-km) Pacific coast, which has some of the best surfing conditions in the world. Mountain climbers test their skills in the country's volcanic ranges. Windsurfing on Lake Arenal, where strong trade winds create ideal conditions, is also popular. Many short and steep-falling rivers have made Costa Rica a worldwide mecca for kayakers and white-water rafters.

## Food

Costa Rican cuisine represents a mix of indigenous and European foods. Potatoes, corn, tomatoes, various fruits, and turkeys are native to Costa Rica. Europeans brought new foods such as beef, pork, and lamb.

Most Costa Rican food revolves around the staples of corn, rice, and beans. Tortillas, flat rounds of cornmeal bread, are often topped with black beans, beef, cheese, and vegetables. Ground corn wrapped in

## PLANTAIN TURNOVERS

A plantain is a long, yellow-green fruit that resembles a banana. In Costa Rica, it is used in a variety of courses for the midday or evening meal, including these filling turnovers.

**4 ripe plantains**
**1 15-ounce can of refried beans
(or ¼ cup shredded Parmesan
cheese )**

**4 tablespoons flour**
**4 tablespoons cooking oil**

1. Peel the ripe plantains and mash them with a fork. Form the mashed plantain into balls, about the size of golf balls.
2. Mix 1 teaspoon of refried beans or cheese into each ball. Roll each ball in 1 teaspoon of flour.
3. Heat oil in a saucepan. Put plantain balls in the hot oil. Fry on each side for 2 to 3 minutes. Serves 2

steamed cornhusks makes up the main ingredient of tamales, which can also be filled with a variety of meats and vegetables and covered with a tomato and chili sauce. The very common dish of *picadillo* contains potatoes or beans with chopped meat, vegetables, peppers, and spices.

A Costa Rican breakfast might include fried eggs, tortillas, rice, and *gallo pinto*, a dish of black beans and rice spiced with peppers, onion, and coriander. The lunchtime dish of *casado* includes a big plate of rice, beans, eggs, pasta, and salad. Dishes of seafood or chicken and rice are usually served in the evening.

The people of the Caribbean coast enjoy a distinct regional cuisine, featuring a lot of coconut milk and coconut oil. Popular Caribbean dishes include coconut custard and coconut-milk-braised shrimp. Afro-Caribbean recipes make frequent use of plantains, cassava (a root that is made into bread and tapioca), breadfruit (a large, round, and starchy fruit), and yams. Guanacaste, the country's principal ranching area, is known for its superior beef, cheese, and milk. People living along the coasts enjoy an abundance of seafood, such as shrimp, lobster, squid, and the Caribbean specialty of conch (the meat of a shelled sea snail).

People often follow their meals with a cup of Costa Rican coffee.

## CACAO BEANS

Cocoa and chocolate are made from the seeds, or beans, of cacao trees. The beans (actually seeds) are found inside pods, which hang from tree trunks and branches. The pods change from green to red as they ripen in the sun. When the pods are ripe, plantation workers cut them down and remove the beans. The beans are dried and then sent to processing plants, where they are ground into a fine brown powder (cocoa) used to make chocolate. To learn more about cacao and to find Costa Rican recipes, visit www.vgsbooks.com for links.

**Cacao beans**

Frescas, or fruit drinks, are made with fruit, cane sugar, and water or milk. Chocolate makes its way into many Costa Rican drinks and desserts, including chocolate candies known as *milanes* and chocolate-topped ice cream cones called *cono capuchinos.* A hot mixture of bittersweet chocolate, milk, sugar, raspberries, and whipped cream is popular along the Caribbean coast.

# THE ECONOMY

In the decades after World War II, Costa Rica remained a stable and—compared to many other Latin American nations—prosperous nation. But much of the country's prosperity was founded on money borrowed from foreign nations, particularly the United States. In the 1980s, the heavy debt load began to have damaging effects. By then one of the most heavily indebted nations in the world, Costa Rica went bankrupt.

Through the 1990s, Costa Rica's economy gradually recovered. A new trend known as ecotourism, in which visitors explore the country's many national parks and wildlife preserves, brought a boom in business. Unemployment declined, and inflation decreased. The economy grew by an average of 5 percent a year, as measured by gross domestic product (GDP—the value of all goods and services produced within Costa Rica in one year).

In the early 2000s, inflation remains relatively stable at about 12 percent a year, while unemployment stands at about 6 percent.

The average worker earns about $4,000 per year. Costa Rica has emerged from its debt crisis and has made new investment to upgrade its telephone system, electric power grid, airports, port facilities, and highways. But money is still tight, and it has been difficult for the government to maintain the good education, health care, and social services that Costa Rica has long provided to its people.

## Agriculture

About 10 percent of Costa Rica's land is arable, or suitable for farming. Agriculture makes up about 9 percent of Costa's Rica's gross domestic product and employs about 20 percent of the workforce.

Coffee production accounts for about 10 percent of all the land under cultivation. Banana production, which reached 2.7 million tons (2.4 metric tons) each year in the early 2000s, remains Costa Rica's most important export business. This fruit is grown on plantations along the Atlantic and Pacific coasts. In recent years, the country has diversified its crops.

## A HEARTY PALM

Pejibaye palm trees produce big clusters of bright yellow, orange, and red fruit that Costa Ricans buy at market stalls and stands along the roadside. The pejibaye is also famous among cooks for the heart of palm, a cluster of tender leaves that are served fresh or cooked by steaming or boiling. The tree's sap can be fermented into an alcoholic drink, its oil can be used in cooking, and its dried fruit can be made into flour.

Farmers cultivate and grow the useful pejibaye on commercial plantations within Costa Rica. Pejibayes are also grown in Hawaii. During the 1990s, hearts of palm cut from Latin American and Hawaiian pejibaye plants found a wide market in the United States.

Costa Rican farmers have increased production of rice, corn, sugarcane, and grain.

Costa Rica also produces and processes cocoa, potatoes, cassava, and a wide variety of fruits, including melons, pineapples, oranges, and palm fruit. Livestock operations raise cattle, pigs, poultry, sheep, goats, and horses. The export of ornamental flowers is a small but growing business, as is the production of sawn timber, industrial wood, and wood for fuel.

Costa Rica processes about 35,000 tons (31,745 metric tons) of fish a year. Small fishing operations on the Pacific coast net tuna, shrimp, and other edible saltwater species. Inland, fish farms produce tilapia and shrimp.

A Costa Rican farmer stands with a mound of pejibaye palm fruit that he has harvested. The fruit will be sold in Central American and U.S. markets.

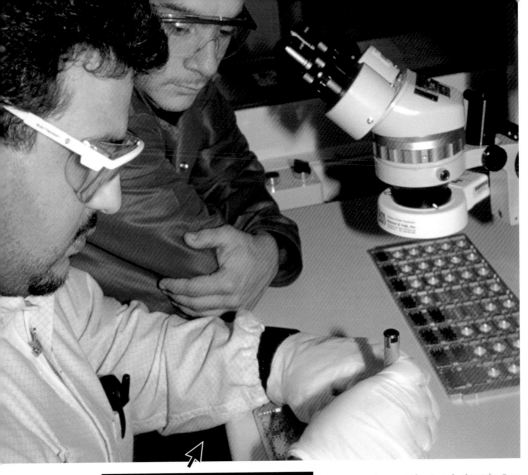

**Technicians assemble microprocessors** for computers at the Intel plant in San José. Intel and other electronics companies came to Costa Rica in the mid-1990s.

## Manufacturing

For many years, industry lagged behind agriculture in Costa Rica. But in the 1980s, taking advantage of cheap labor costs, many new companies set up businesses in Costa Rica. Also in the 1980s, Costa Rica opened free-trade zones in the Central Valley. In these zones, companies could operate without paying import taxes. The free-trade zones helped manufacturing become the largest contributor to Costa Rica's GDP. Many industrial businesses are foreign-owned.

In the early 2000s, industry accounts for about 37 percent of the country's GDP and employs about 22 percent of all workers. Costa Rican factories produce medicines, spare parts for cars and buses, clothing, cigarettes, fuels, cement, and chemicals. A large textile industry exports its goods to the United States and Europe. Food processing—the preparation and packaging of meat, vegetables, fruit, and fish—is an important industry, with many products used locally and not exported. Fertilizer plants supply Costa Rican farms with phosphates, nitrogen, and organic wastes. Several large foreign-owned companies operate high-technology plants, which make microprocessors used in computers and telecommunications equipment.

# Services and Tourism

Service industries, such as banking, sales, and tourism, employ about six out of every ten Costa Ricans and make up the largest economic sector in Costa Rica, accounting for about 54 percent of the nation's GDP. Large accounting firms, banks, and insurance companies have headquarters in San José and local branches in other important cities. Shopping malls are also found in major cities. There, working-class and middle-class Costa Ricans can browse through a wide selection of clothing, electronics, and appliances. The service industry also includes fast-food operations.

In the late twentieth century, tourism exploded and became one of Costa Rica's busiest industries. More than 1 million visitors come to Costa Rica each year, and they bring about $1.2 billion to the Costa Rican economy, almost 10 percent of the country's total GDP. Several factors brought about the growth in tourism, welcomed by government officials as a stable, profitable, and relatively trouble-free way of earning money. First, Costa Rica's extensive system of national parks and nature preserves has attracted ecotourists—travelers who want to observe tropical wildlife in its natural state. Ecotourism, in turn, has given rise to hotels, resorts, guide companies, travel agencies, and other travel-related businesses. Costa Rica's political stability has also attracted tourists, who do not want to visit its strife-torn Central American neighbors, such as Nicaragua and El Salvador.

Costa Rica's rich and varied environment brings many **tourists** and dollars into the country each year. Arenal Volcano *(above)* is a popular destination for many visitors to Costa Rica.

These Costa Rican women are **preparing bananas for export** to world markets. Shipping millions of boxes of bananas each year, Costa Rica is the second largest exporter of bananas in the world.

The new tourist businesses provide employment to Costa Rican workers, who help operate the visitor accommodations and services. Many poor and isolated locales, including areas once limited to small farms and fishing, have benefited from the boom. Nevertheless, tourism has given rise to a debate over the pros and cons of economic development. New resort buildings litter many once-pristine coastal areas, while the crowds of visitors to natural parks can damage fragile ecosystems (communities of interdependent plants and animals). In addition, many tourist businesses are owned by foreigners and foreign companies. When such businesses buy land for tourist development, they drive up prices, making land and homes too expensive for ordinary Costa Rican families.

## Foreign Trade

Foreign trade makes up a vital aspect of the Costa Rican economy. The country relies on exports to bring in money and on imports to provide many of the basic foodstuffs and necessities of life for its people. The United States has long been Costa Rica's principal trading partner, accounting for a little more than half of all imports and exports. Costa Rica's principal Latin American trading partners are Mexico, Guatemala, and Venezuela. About 25 percent of Costa Rican exports and 10 percent of imports are exchanged with European countries.

The country's principal exports are coffee, bananas, pineapples, beef, textiles, electronic equipment, and sugar. Costa Rica imports raw materials for manufacturing and construction, heavy equipment, transportation equipment, oil, and consumer goods.

In 1994 Costa Rica signed a free-trade agreement with Mexico, one of the largest nations in Latin America. This treaty forged closer political and economic links between the two nations. Costa Rica also actively takes part in the World Trade Organization, which it joined in 1994 as an original founding member. Currently in the planning stages is a free-trade zone throughout the Americas. This zone will boost foreign trade for Costa Rica and other nations and foster new business investment.

## Transportation

Costa Rica has about 22,370 miles (36,000 km) of roads, but only about 3,728 miles (6,000 km) are paved. The best roads are found in the cities of the Central Valley. Mountainous areas commonly have only narrow, winding, and usually unpaved tracks, frequently blocked by rockfalls and mud slides. In more level areas, bicycles, carts, motorcycles, trucks, buses, and private cars jam narrow highways. The Pan-American Highway (which runs the length of Latin America) is known in Costa Rica as the Interamericana. It runs north-south through Costa Rica, passing through San José and other principal cities of the Central Valley.

San José provides the hub for air and land transportation in Costa Rica. The nation's principal airport, the Juan Santamaría International Airport, lies between San José and Alajuela. Two domestic airlines provide flights from there to cities in the Nicoya Peninsula, Puntarenas Province, and Caribbean coast. International carriers link San José with North America, Europe, and South America.

Public bus lines provide transportation for the large number of Costa Ricans who don't have their own cars. Residents and tourists on the Nicoya and Oso peninsulas can take a car ferry to the mainland, a service that cuts several hours from the journey over land.

## The Future

Costa Rica has entered the twenty-first century with a stabilizing economy, although one still burdened by debt. The tradition of public ownership of vital businesses and state-supported social services often throws the government budget into deficit. In turn, government deficits weaken the currency and affect the banking system. In addition, low government investment in roads, bridges, electricity, and telecommunications systems hinders economic activity. Nevertheless, diversified agriculture is providing a growing amount of export earnings. Poverty has declined, while a large middle class provides a buffer against social tensions. This stability attracts foreign investment, which creates jobs and exporting industries.

The tourist industry in Costa Rica remains a success, but it has given rise to a debate on environmental costs. New resorts and hotels need land, water, and other natural resources. These developments replace productive farmland and also destroy natural habitat. At some point, Costa Rica may slow or halt tourist developments for the sake of preserving its remaining land in a natural state.

Costa Rica's prospects remain bright. Through long tradition, the country has achieved a stable democracy, one that encourages public participation. Costa Ricans make a national celebration of their elections, with schoolchildren even casting votes of their own (although their votes don't count). In recent years, some Costa Ricans have grown unhappy with their leaders' policies and with the dominance of the two major political parties. Still, the people of this nation take pride in their tradition of open democracy and free and fair elections. With much of Latin America going through political turmoil and economic hard times, Costa Rica has a long head start on a stable and prosperous future.

## CHILDREN WHO WORK

On Costa Rica's extensive coffee plantations, some of the workers are children. Valued for their small size and nimble fingers, many children help harvest coffee beans in November and December. Some are the children of illegal immigrants from Nicaragua. By working in the coffee fields, they help their families earn extra money. A coffee picker earns about one dollar for every bucket of beans picked, a task that takes about an hour.

Under a law passed in 1998, children between the ages of fifteen and eighteen may work in Costa Rica, but they are also required to attend school when school is in session. Children younger than fifteen can also work, but they must be registered with the government. More than 100,000 Costa Rican children hold jobs on coffee plantations and in other businesses.

Learn more about the Costa Rican economy at www.vgsbooks.com, where you'll find links to websites featuring import and export figures, the banana and coffee industries, and a currency converter.

**Timeline**

**12,000 B.C.** Human settlement of Costa Rica begins.

**1000 B.C.** Permanent settlements thrive in Costa Rica's Central Valley.

**200 B.C.** Native artisans begin to carve granodiorite into perfect spheres, perhaps used as religious or astronomical markers.

**A.D. 1400** The large city of Guayabo is abandoned or destroyed during conflict between indigenous tribes of the Central Highlands.

**1502** Christopher Columbus explores the Caribbean coast of present-day Costa Rica.

**1522** Captain Gil González Dávila leads an exploration of Costa Rica's interior.

**1539** Convinced the region holds gold, Spanish explorers dub the territory Costa Rica, or "rich coast."

**1563** Explorer Juan Vásquez de Coronado establishes the town of Cartago in the Central Valley.

**1570** The Captaincy General of Guatemala is founded. Costa Rica becomes part of this political unit.

**1630s** Costa Ricans in Cartago build their first shrine to the Virgin Mary (the biblical mother of Jesus). Destroyed by an earthquake, the shrine is later replaced by the Basilica of Our Lady of the Angels, a church.

**CA. 1738** San José is founded.

**1808** The first coffee plants arrive in Costa Rica from Jamaica.

**1821** The nations of Central America declare themselves independent of Spain.

**1825** The province of Guanacaste is annexed to Costa Rica.

**1838** The United Provinces of Central America is dissolved.

**1856** Costa Rican troops defeat a mercenary army led by William Walker; Juan Santamaría is shot while setting fire to an enemy fort, making him a national hero.

**1888** The U.S.-based United Fruit Company arrives in Costa Rica to build banana plantations on the Caribbean coast.

**1890** The Atlantic Railway, linking San José to the Caribbean coast, is completed.

**1917** President Alfredo González Flores is ousted in a coup led by Federico Tinoco, the minister of war.

**1934** A strike against the United Fruit Company succeeds in winning the support of the Costa Rican government and some improvements for workers.

**1948** Costa Rica suffers forty-four days of civil war after a contested presidential election.

**1949** A new constitution grants citizenship and voting rights to all Costa Rican adults, except Indians.

**1971** The Costa Rican government sets up twenty-two indigenous reserves, areas set aside for use by native peoples.

**1987** President Oscar Arias Sánchez is awarded the Nobel Peace Prize for his efforts in negotiating a general peace accord in Central America.

**1991** Costa Rican Indians win full citizenship and the right to vote.

**1998** The Costa Rican author Carmen Naranjo is nominated for a Nobel Prize for Literature.

**2002** Abel Pacheco—a Costa Rican literary and media celebrity—wins a runoff election to become president.

**2004** After several years of negotiations with the United States and Central American nations, the Costa Rican government signs the Central American Free Trade Agreement (CAFTA).

**COUNTRY NAME** Republic of Costa Rica

**AREA** 19,929 square miles (51,616 sq. km)

**MAIN LANDFORMS** Caribbean Lowlands, Central Valley, Central Range, Guanacaste Range, Tilarán Range, Talamanca Range, Nicoya Peninsula, Osa Peninsula, Barva Volcano, Arenal Volcano, Irazú Volcano, Poás Volcano, Tenorio Volcano

**HIGHEST POINT** Chirripó Grande, 12,530 feet ( 3,819 m) above sea level

**LOWEST POINT** sea level

**MAJOR RIVERS** Chirripó, Chirripó Atlántico, Estrella, General, Pacuare, Reventazón, San Juan, Sixaola, Tempisque, Tenorio

**ANIMALS** deer, monkeys, ocelots, coyotes, pelicans, raccoons, sea turtles, boa constrictors, tanagers, crocodiles, iguanas, pumas, anteaters, sloths, jaguars, eagles, toucans, parakeets, ospreys, owls, herons, storks

**CAPITAL CITY** San José

**OTHER MAJOR CITIES** Alajuela, Heredia, Cartago, Puerto Limón

**OFFICIAL LANGUAGE** Spanish

**MONETARY UNIT** Colon. 100 centimos = 1 colon.

## COSTA RICA'S CURRENCY

The currency of Costa Rica is known as the colon. It is named for explorer Christopher Columbus, whose name in Spanish is Cristóbal Colón. Each colon is divided into 100 centimos. Costa Rica issues bills (paper money) in denominations of 20, 50, 100, 500, 1,000, 2,000, 5,000, and 10,000 colons and coins worth 1, 2, 5, 10, 20, 25, and 100 colons. About 400 colons equal one U.S. dollar.

The flag of Costa Rica was designed in 1848 by Pacífica Fernández Oreamuno, the wife of Costa Rica's president. It displays five horizontal bands. From top to bottom, the bands are blue, white, red, white, and blue. The blue stands for the sky and for the country's intellectual and religious spirit. White stands for peace. Red stands for the blood shed for independence. In formal settings, such as schools and government offices, the flag includes the country's coat of arms, set in a white disk on the flag's red stripe. The coat of arms includes seven stars, each one standing for a province. The sun rises on the horizon above two oceans, the Pacific and the Caribbean. Two ships, representing Costa Rican commerce, sail these oceans. Three volcanoes rise up from a green island, standing for Costa Rica and its mountain ranges and volcanoes.

Costa Rica's national anthem is "Noble Patria, Tu Hermosa Bandera" ("Noble Homeland, Your Beautiful Flag"). The music was written in 1852 by orchestra director Manuel María Gutiérrez. In 1903 the government held a contest to search for suitable words for the music. The winner was José María Zeledón. The complete anthem with words and music was first performed on September 15, 1903. Here are two verses from the national anthem in English:

### Noble Homeland, Your Beautiful Flag
Noble country, our lives
Are revealed in your flying flag;
For in peace, white and pure, we live tranquil
Beneath the clear limpid blue of your sky.
..............................................................

Oh, sweet country, our refuge and shelter;
How fertile your life giving soil!
May your people contented and peaceful
Unmolested continue their hard work.

For a link to a website where you can listen to the Costa Rican national anthem, "Noble Homeland, Your Beautiful Flag," visit www.vgsbooks.com.

**Flag** · **National Anthem**

**OSCAR ARIAS SÁNCHEZ** (b. 1941) Born in Heredia and president of Costa Rica from 1986 to 1990, Arias emerged as a leader of the National Liberation Party after the retirement of José Figueres Ferrer. Arias played an important role in mediating the 1980s conflict between Communist and anti-Communist factions in neighboring Nicaragua and throughout Central America. The Arias Plan, which he devised, earned him the Nobel Peace Prize in 1987.

**RAFAEL ANGEL CALDERÓN GUARDIA** (1900–1970) Born in Diriamba, Nicaragua, Calderón became a member of the Costa Rican landowning class as an adult and was elected president of Costa Rica in 1940. He enacted a number of reforms that helped Costa Rican workers, including an increase in wages and the right to strike for better working conditions. In 1943 Calderón's government supported a strike by banana workers against the United Fruit Company. After bitterly contested elections and civil war in 1948, Calderón was exiled from Costa Rica by the new leader, José Figueres Ferrer.

**QUINCE DUNCAN** (b. 1940) Born in San José, Duncan is a black Costa Rican novelist who struggled against racial prejudice in his youth. He obtained graduate degrees in literature and linguistics at the national university in San José. He went on to write stories and novels describing the unique Afro-Caribbean community of Costa Rica's eastern coast. Many of his stories have been published in *The Best Short Stories of Quince Duncan.*

**JOSÉ "PEPE" FIGUERES FERRER** (1906–1987) Founder of the National Liberation Party, Figueres was born in San Ramón and grew up to emerge as Costa Rica's most important political figure after the 1948 civil war. Figueres was a driving force behind the 1949 constitution, which is still in effect, and the modern administration of Costa Rica. He is remembered for abolishing the Costa Rican army and extending citizenship and voting rights to almost all Costa Ricans. He served as president from 1953 to 1957 and again from 1970 to 1974.

**CARMEN LYRA** (1888–1949) The first prominent female writer in Costa Rica, Lyra was born in San José. She helped found the Costa Rican Communist Party in 1931. Lyra wrote in a style called socialist realism, drawing her characters from workers and the poor to point out social inequalities in Costa Rican society. Some of her most famous works are *Tales of My Aunt Panchita, Bananas and Men,* and *The Golden Bean.*

Famous People

**CARMEN NARANJO** (b. 1928) Born in Cartago, Naranjo has published novels, plays, short stories, essays, and poetry. She was nominated for a Nobel Prize for Literature in 1998. Naranjo served as Costa Rica's culture minister in the 1970s and helped found the National Theater and the National Symphony Orchestra. *There Never Was a Once Upon a Time*, a book of short stories, is one of her well known works.

**ABEL PACHECO** (b. 1937) Leader of the Social Christian Unity Party, Pacheco was born in San José. He was elected Costa Rica's president in 2002. Pacheco grew up in Limón Province on Costa Rica's Caribbean coast. He went into exile after Costa Rica's civil war in 1948. After studying medicine in Mexico, he returned to Costa Rica and became director of the National Psychiatric Hospital. Later, he operated a successful clothing factory in Costa Rica, then became a poet and well-known television commentator.

**CLAUDIA POLL** (b. 1972) Born in Managua, Nicaragua, Poll later moved to Costa Rica. A competitive swimmer, she won Costa Rica's first Olympic gold medal, in the 200-meter freestyle, at the 1996 Summer Games in Atlanta, Georgia. At the Games in Sydney, Australia, in 2000, Poll won bronze medals in the 200-meter and 400-meter freestyle, the only medals won by Costa Rica that year.

**JUAN SANTAMARÍA** (ca. 1836–1856) Born in Alajuela, Santamaría was a young volunteer in the Costa Rican army that gathered to oppose an invasion by mercenary forces under the control of U.S. adventurer William Walker. At the Battle of Rivas in 1856, Santamaría bravely set fire to an enemy fortification but was killed in the action. The battle forced Walker's troops to retreat from Costa Rica and turned Santamaría into a national hero.

**FRANCISCO ZUÑIGA** (1912–1998) Zuñiga was a San José–born artist who celebrated the lives of ordinary working people in his bronze sculptures. Many of Zuñiga's sculptures decorate public squares and parks in Costa Rica. He also made prints and paintings.

**LAS BAULAS DE GUANACASTE NATIONAL MARINE PARK** This marine park (covering both beaches, swamps, and ocean) lies along the Pacific coast in northwestern Costa Rica. It is best known as home to the leatherback turtles of Playa Grande. During the nesting season, from October to March, these sea turtles waddle ashore to lay their eggs. At the height of the season, more than two thousand separate nests dot the sands of Playa Grande.

**GUAYABO NATIONAL MONUMENT** The monument marks the site of a large pre-Columbian (pre-European) city, which dates to about 1000 B.C., in Cartago Province. The city survives in the form of stone houses, terraces, walkways, and aqueducts. Petroglyphs, or carvings on large stones and cliff faces, also can be seen here.

**IRAZÚ VOLCANO** The highest active volcano of Central America, reaching an elevation of 11,259 feet (3,432 m), lies at the center of the Irazú Volcano National Park. The volcano's last major eruption took place on March 19, 1963. Pillars of smoke still drift up from Irazú's two main craters.

**MONTEVERDE CLOUD FOREST PRESERVE** This 26,000-acre (10,530-hectare) park is located about 60 miles (100 km) northwest of San José. The preserve offers rope ladders, harnesses, platforms, and a series of wooden bridges, allowing visitors to tour the forest canopy, the tangle of sprawling branches and vines at treetop level. Donations collected from schools worldwide helped establish the nearby Children's Eternal Rainforest, a 50,000-acre (20,250-hectare) private biological reserve.

**SAN JOSÉ** Visitors to San José, Costa Rica's capital city, can enjoy a variety of urban activities. They can see operas, dance performances, and concerts at the Teatro Nacional (the National Theater), learn about Costa Rican history, culture, and geology at the Museo Nacional (the National Museum), and view ancient carvings, coins, and artworks at the Museo de Oro (the Museum of Gold). San José also offers a lively nightlife, including plentiful movie theaters and fine restaurants. Those who like soccer can even see world-class competition at the Estadio Nacional (the National Stadium).

**SANTA ROSA NATIONAL PARK** Founded in 1971, this was the first of Costa Rica's national parks. Located in the northwestern part of Costa Rica, the park covers 122,000 acres (49,373 hectares). The park provides research facilities for scientists studying its tropical ecosystems. It also includes the Hacienda Santa Rosa, the site of a famous battle between Costa Rican soldiers and William Walker's mercenaries in 1856.

**archaeologist:** a scholar who studies the remains of past human cultures

**canopy:** a top layer of tree leaves and branches that creates a covering over the forest plants below

**cloud forest:** a high-altitude rain forest covered in clouds year-round

**colony:** a community of immigrants who settle a new land but still follow the laws and government of their homeland

**communism:** a political philosophy that banishes private property and places the state in direct control of the national economy

**dictatorship:** rule by a single person, who usually does not allow dissent or opposition

**ecosystem:** an interdependent community of plants and animals

**encomienda:** A rural estate granted to a Spanish colonist. The colonist was also given the right to use the labor of local indigenous people and was expected to oversee their conversion to Christianity.

**erosion:** the wearing away of soil or rock by wind, rain, ice, or flowing water

**extinction:** the death of an entire species of plant, insect, or animal

**free trade zone:** areas where businesses can operate without paying import taxes. Free trade zones encourage foreign trade.

**gross domestic product (GDP):** a measure of the total value of goods and services produced within a country during a certain amount of time (usually one year)

**habitat:** the natural home of a plant or animal

**inflation:** a decrease in the value of money, which brings about higher prices

**mestizo:** a person of mixed Indian and European ancestry

**nationalize:** to make assets—businesses, natural resources, or land—the property of the government

**oligarchy:** rule by a small group of wealthy and powerful people

**patron saint:** among Catholics, a historical figure sainted by the Church and believed to protect a family or community from disease and misfortune

**pilgrimage:** a journey to a religious shrine or holy place

**privatize:** to sell state-owned assets, such as banks and businesses, to private owners and foreign investors

**rain forest:** a complex ecosystem of trees, plants, and animals that thrive in humidity and heavy rainfall

**shaman:** in indigenous societies, a religious leader who uses the magical properties of plants, animals, and unseen spirits to heal injuries and illness

**social security:** a system of medical services, unemployment insurance, and retirement benefits designed to help the neediest members of society

Glossary

Biesanz, Mavis Hiltunen, Richard Biesanz, and Karen Zubris Biesanz. *The Ticos: Culture and Social Change in Costa Rica.* Boulder, CO: Lynne Reinner Publishers, 1998.
The authors draw on their own experiences of living in Costa Rica, as well as extensive interviews with native Costa Ricans, to portray the history, culture, religion, working life, families, and style of the country.

Calderon, Gloria. *The Life of Costa Rica.* Bogotá, Colombia: Villegas Editores, 2001.
Calderon, a professor of photojournalism, offers more than three hundred photographs depicting daily life, work, and play in Costa Rica. Illuminating text accompanies the photographs.

Gudmundson, Lowell. *Costa Rica before Coffee: Society and Economy on the Eve of the Export Boom.* Baton Rouge: Louisiana State University Press, 1986.
Gudmundson presents a scholarly essay on the effect of the coffee trade on Costa Rican agriculture and society. He argues that, rather than creating a privileged class of landowner/planters, coffee actually helped Costa Rica achieve a more democratic society.

Haber, Harvey, ed. *Costa Rica.* Boston: Houghton Mifflin, 1993.
Part of the Insight Guides series, this book for visitors includes a historical and political background on Costa Rica.

Helmuth, Chalene. *Culture and Customs of Costa Rica.* Westport, CT: Greenwood Press, 2000.
This guidebook describes the arts, literature, religion, language, food, and other aspects of modern Costa Rican society.

Lara, Silvia, Tom Barry, and Peter Simonson. *Inside Costa Rica: The Essential Guide to Its Politics, Economy, Society, and Environment.* Albuquerque, NM: Resource Center Press, 1995.
This detailed book on modern Costa Rica delves into economic news of the 1980s and early 1990s and offers extensive discussion of environmental issues.

Longley, Kyle. *The Sparrow and the Hawk: Costa Rica and the United States during the Rise of José Figueres.* Tuscaloosa: University of Alabama Press, 1997.
The author describes the economic and political relationship of Costa Rica and the United States and explains reasons for U.S. support of the Figueres coup and presidency.

Molina, Ivan Jimenez. *The History of Costa Rica: Brief, Up-to-Date, and Illustrated.* San José: Editorial de la Universidad de Costa Rica, 1998.
This short survey of Costa Rican history, originally published in Spanish, presents recent events from a Costa Rican perspective.

**Rachowiecki, Rob.** *Costa Rica.* **Footscray, Australia: Lonely Planet Publications, 2002.**
This guidebook for tourists explores many unknown and out-of-the-way towns and sites in Costa Rica.

**Schafer, Kevin, and Alvaro Ugalde.** *Costa Rica: The Forests of Eden.* **New York: Rizzoli, 1996.**
This striking book of color photographs taken in the rain forests of Costa Rica shows flora and fauna in rich detail. Helpful and informative text explains the workings of the rain forest ecosystem as well as current environmental issues.

### Further Reading and Websites

*AM Costa Rica*
<http://www.amcostarica.com/>
This daily English-language newspaper from San José offers a host of information about current events in Costa Rica.

**Collard, Sneed B. *Monteverde: Science and Scientists in a Costa Rican Cloud Forest*. New York: Franklin Watts, 2003.**
This book explores Costa Rica's Monteverde Cloud Forest Preserve and the research of scientists who study its plants, animals, trees, and habitat.

*CostaRica.com*
<http://www.costarica.com/>
This general-interest site includes discussion forums, chat rooms, classified advertising, and a Costa Rica Internet Community, Kitchen, and Trading (CRICKT) section allowing exchange of ideas and information on the country.

*Costa Rica Tourism Board*
<http://www.visitcostarica.com/>
This site offers news, statistics, information, and a photo gallery of Costa Rican attractions, designed for foreign visitors.

**Dobles, Fabian. *Years Like Brief Days*. Chester Springs, PA: Dufour Editions, 1995.**
This novel by a Costa Rican novelist describes the return of an elderly man to the village of his childhood, and his painful memories of parents, school, and friends.

**Foley, Erin. *Costa Rica*. New York: Marshall Cavendish, 1997.**
This book for young readers offers a description of Costa Rican geography, with sections on history, government, the arts, and entertainment.

**Henderson, Aileen Kilgore. *The Monkey Thief*. Minneapolis: Milkweed Editions, 1997.**
In this story, a young boy from Minnesota is sent to live in Costa Rica. He discovers the weird and sometimes frightening world of the tropical rain forest.

*Instituto Nacional de Bioversidad (Institute of National Biodiversity)*
<http://www.inbio.ac.cr/en/default.html>
This site is devoted to the issues of biodiversity and the preservation of natural habitat in Costa Rica.

**Morrison, Marion. *Costa Rica*. New York: Children's Press, 1998.**
This book offers an introduction to Costa Rican society, history, economics, and culture.

**Patent, Dorothy Hinshaw. *Biodiversity*. New York: Clarion Books, 1996.**
The author describes the rich plant and animal life of the rain forests of Costa Rica as well as North America. She explains basic concepts and issues, including natural selection, species, extinction, and habitat preservation.

**Ras, Barbara, and Oscar Arias, eds.** *Costa Rica: A Traveler's Literary Companion.* **San Francisco: Whereabouts Press, 1994.**
This anthology presents twenty-six short stories by Costa Rican writers, each describing a particular region of the country.

### Tico Times Online Edition
**<http://www.ticotimes.net/>**
Billing itself as the leading daily English newspaper of Central America, the *Tico Times* posts this website with business and tourism information, listings of cultural events, and news reports.

### vgsbooks.com
**<http://www.vgsbooks.com>**
Visit www.vgsbooks.com, the home page of the Visual Geography Series®. You can get linked to all sorts of useful on-line information, including geographical, historical, demographic, cultural, and economic websites. The www.vgs books.com site is a great resource for late-breaking news and statistics.

lakes, 9, 10, 14, 16, 56
language, 4, 21, 40, 42, 46–47, 68
Lyra, Carmen, 47–48, 70

manufacturing, 41, 61, 63
mestizos, 5, 40, 41, 73
Mexico, 21, 24, 25, 26, 52, 63, 64
Miskitos, 26, 28
mountains, 9–10, 13, 21, 68
movies, 49–50
museums, 17, 18, 22, 72
music, 48–49, 50, 51

Naranjo, Carmen, 48, 66, 70
National Liberation Party (PLN), 33, 34, 35, 37, 70
national parks and preserves, 7, 10, 13, 14, 16–17, 58, 62, 72
natural resources, 15
Nicaragua, 9, 24, 26, 27, 29, 34, 55, 62, 65, 70, 71

Pacheco, Abel, 35, 66, 70–71
Pacto de Concordia, 27
Panama, 9, 10, 12, 16, 39, 48
Patti, Adelina, 50
Poll, Claudia, 71
population, 10
Puerto Limón, 19, 41, 42, 68

radio, 51
rainfall, 9, 12–13
rain forests, 8, 9, 14, 15, 16, 17, 50, 72, 73. *See also* forests and forestry
recipe, 56
religion, 21, 22, 39, 53–54
rivers, 9, 12, 14, 15, 16, 68
roads, 5, 28, 29, 64

San José, 10, 16, 17–18, 22, 27, 43, 49, 50, 64, 68, 70; founding of, 25, 66; and government, 28, 31, 37
Santamaría, Juan, 18–19, 29, 66, 71
Santa Rosa National Park, 17, 72
sculpture, 52, 71
service industry, 62–63
shamans, 21, 39, 54, 73
slaves and slavery, 5, 24, 25, 26, 27, 42

soccer, 55–56
Social Christian Unity Party (PUSC), 35, 37, 70
social services, 7, 32, 33, 44–45, 59, 64
Solís, Ottón, 35
Spanish settlers, 5, 23–26, 40
sports, 50, 51, 55–56, 71. *See also* Poll, Claudia
Supreme Tribunal, 33, 36

taxes, 28, 29, 31, 33, 50, 61
telephones, 17, 51, 59
television, 50
theater, 17, 50, 70
Tinoco Granados, Federico, 31, 66
tourism, 39, 51, 58, 72; and environmental problems, 7, 13, 15, 62–63, 65
trade, 26, 28, 31, 41, 61, 63–64
transportation, 29, 30, 59, 64

United Fruit Company, 29, 31–32, 48, 66, 70
United Provinces of Central America, 27, 28, 66
United States, 19, 29, 30, 31, 50, 54, 58, 60, 61, 63, 66, 71

volcanoes, 9, 10, 19, 25, 50, 62, 72
voters and voting, 27, 30, 33, 34, 35, 36, 37, 40, 42, 65, 66, 70

Walker, William, 19, 29, 54, 66, 71, 72
War of National Liberation, 32–33
War of the League, 28
women, 30
World Bank, 34
World Trade Organization, 64
World War I, 31
World War II, 54, 58
writers and writing, 46, 47–48, 52, 70

Zuñiga, Francisco, 52, 71

**Captions for photos appearing on cover and chapter openers:**

Cover: Steam rises from the crater lake of Poás Volcano, located in Costa Rica's Central Range. Volcanic activity within the mountain creates the deadly steam. Visit www.vgsbooks.com for links to information about Costa Rica's volcanoes.

pp. 4–5 The Pacific Ocean meets lush rain forest along the coast of Costa Rica's Puntarenas Province.

pp. 8–9 Clouds envelop the Monteverde Cloud Forest Preserve in Costa Rica's Tilarán Range. Cloud forests are a special kind of rain forest located in tropical mountain regions. The altitude of cloud forests places them directly within clouds much of the time. Visit www.vgsbooks.com for more information.

pp. 20–21 The stone foundations and streets of Guayabo National Monument poke through the vegetation of the Central Range. Costa Rican Indians built this ancient city located on the southern slope of Turrialba Volcano (near Irazú Volcano) about three thousand years ago. At its peak, from A.D. 400 to 1400, the city was home to as many as ten thousand residents. It is not clear why the city went into decline and residents abandoned the city shortly after 1400. For more information about the Guayabo ruins, visit www.vgsbooks.com.

pp. 38–39 Costa Ricans walk along San José's Avenida Central (Central Avenue), which is open to pedestrians only. San José is home to 309,672 of Costa Rica's roughly 4 million citizens.

pp. 46–47 This artwork is from a traditional Costa Rican painted *carreta*, or oxcart, from the village of Sarchí. The oxcart was once the only way for Costa Ricans to transport coffee beans to market. The colorful designs on the oxcarts were symbols of pride, showing the region from which the growers and their coffee came. To learn more, visit www.vgsbooks.com.

pp. 58–59 A young worker picks coffee beans during the coffee harvest (November to January) in Costa Rica's Central Valley region. Many schools in Costa Rica hold break during the harvest season to allow students to help their families gather the coffee crop.

**Photo Acknowledgments**

The images in this book are used with the permission of: © kevinschafer.com, pp. 4–5, 8–9, 10, 12, 13, 14 (left), 17, 46–47, 62; Ron Bell/Digital Cartographics, pp. 6, 11; Courtesy Costa Rica Tourism Board, pp. 7, 15 (top and bottom), 25, 52 (right), 55; © Robert Fried, pp. 14 (right), 40, 60; © John Mitchell, pp. 18–19, 22, 51, 57; © Dave G. Houser/CORBIS, pp. 20–21; courtesy of the Library of Congress, pp. 23 (LC-USZ62-51767), 30 (LC-USZ62-42288); © Bettmann/CORBIS, pp. 27, 32, 33; © CORBIS, p. 29; © Reuters NewMedia Inc./CORBIS, pp. 35, 36; © Robert Francis/South American Pictures, pp. 38–39; © Victor Englebert, pp. 41, 52 (left), 58–59; © Diane Cooper, p. 43; © Martin Rogers/CORBIS, p. 44; photo by Dr. Roma Hoff, pp. 49, 63; © Larry Luxner/Luxner News Inc., pp. 60–61; © Todd Strand/Independent Picture Service, p. 68.

Cover photo: © kevinschafer.com. Back cover: NASA.